FIERCE GOODBYE

LIVING IN THE SHADOW OF SUICIDE

by
G. LLOYD CARR

with poetry by
GWENDOLYN C. CARR

**Herald
Press**

Scottdale, Pennsylvania
Waterloo, Ontario

Library of Congress Cataloging-in-Publication Data
Carr, G. Lloyd, 1930-
  Fierce goodbye : living in the shadow of suicide / by G. Lloyd Carr ;
with poetry by Gwendolyn C. Carr.
      p. cm.
Rev. ed. of the work originally published under title: After the storm.
Includes bibliographical references and index.
  ISBN 0-8361-9267-2 (pbk. : alk. paper)
    1. Suicide–Religious aspects–Christianity. 2. Suicide–United States–
Case studies. 3. Suicide victims–United States–Family relationships–
Case studies. I. Carr, Gwendolyn C. II. Carr, G. Lloyd, 1930- After
the storm. III. Title.
  HV6545.C264 2004
  248.8'66—dc22   2003023012

FIERCE GOODBYE
Copyright © 2004 G. Lloyd Carr and Gwendolyn Carr
Published by Herald Press, Scottdale, Pa. 15683 and simultaneously in
    Canada by Herald Press, Waterloo, Ont. N2L 6H7. All rights
    reserved
Library of Congress Catalog Card Number: 2003023012
International Standard Book Number: 0-8361-9267-2
Printed in the United States of America

12 11 10 09 08 07 06 05   10 9 8 7 6 5 4 3 2

To order or request information, please call
1-800-759-4447 (individuals); 1-800-245-7894 (trade).
Website: www.heraldpress.com

TO
REV. JAMES R. HAY,
PASTOR, BROTHER, COLLEAGUE, FRIEND,
WHO WAS THERE WHEN WE NEEDED HIM.

CONTENTS

The 30,000 suicides each year in the United States, while horrific by themselves, form part of a larger story of seldom-recognized pain and devastation. For every person who dies by suicide, at least six close family members and friends are left to mourn. Further impacted are the churches and social communities in which suicides take place, and in which the survivors must try to rebalance their lives—communities often ill-equipped to provide needed support.

By some estimates, one out of every six individuals mourns the loss of a family member or friend who has died by suicide, has had serious suicidal thoughts themselves, or is a caregiver of someone who does. Ninety to ninety-five percent of suicides are attributable to a handful of mental illnesses, all of which are highly treatable. Yet the tragedy continues.

While there are many resources aimed at preventing suicide, there are far fewer resources for survivors of suicide. These survivors face a shattered world of anger, guilt, and grief. Grief is a lonely affair, made lonelier by the silence of family, friends, and church.

Through the documentary, *Fierce Goodbye: Living in the Shadow of Suicide*, Mennonite Media, in cooperation with Faith and Values Media, lifts up the plight of those living in the shadow of suicide. The title for the documentary arose from the production team reading Lloyd and Gwendolyn Carr's book by a similar title. As survivors of suicide, the Carrs write compassionately about their experience. We are grateful for their insights and permission to allow us to use their title.

Through interviews with mental health experts, theologians, and with the families and friends of those who have died by suicide, the documentary places the difficulties of those living in the aftermath of suicide squarely before the public's eye.

Herald Press has graciously agreed to bring this book into circulation as a special documentary video edition. It will stand as an additional resource for those living in the shadow of suicide.

—Burton Buller, producer of *Fierce Goodbye: Living in the Shadow of Suicide*

HANGING ON

It's hard to pin this anxious hope
on one remaining star,
and harder
when you realize it's flung
a million miles.

But hope hangs on to anything
glimmering in the night.
Any beckoning stab of light
unpins all anxiety.

Early in the morning of December 9, 1983, our daughter-in-law, Katrina[1] died violently of a self-inflicted gunshot wound. She was less than three months past her thirtieth birthday.

Our only child is a son, which made Katie more than a daughter-in-law—she was the daughter we never had. This is not her story, someone else must tell that. This is not our son's story nor our grandson's. Rob and Josh must tell their own stories in their own way and in their own time. Nor is this a theological or psychological investigation into the reasons or causes that led up to her final act. Examining those areas may be of interest to theologians or psychologists researching depression or pre-suicidal behavior, but that sort of study does nothing to ease the burden of grief. Rather, what we have tried to do in this account is to record some of the things the two of us shared in those first few months which helped us through early stages of mourning, in the hope that we may be able to help others who share similar bereavement.

Sometime in the late spring or early summer of 1984, Pastor Jim said to me, "I hope you are going to do something to share how you two have survived through all this." Gwen had already begun to use her poetry to work out her despair and sorrow, but at that time I was too caught up in my own grief to respond with more than the usual platitudes. However, by autumn the book began to take shape in my mind, and I began some preliminary work on it during the winter and early spring of 1985. Then, because of very heavy teaching and administrative demands during the 1986-1988 college terms, I had to set it aside. As a result, the manuscript was not completed until the autumn of 1988 during a sabbatical spent at Tyndale House in Cambridge, England.

I want to express my thanks to the Faculty Development Committee and the Senate of Gordon College for providing partial funding and granting the sabbatical leave which gave me the time to complete the project. The staff at Tyndale House, particularly the warden, Bruce Winter, and the librarian, David Deboys, have been extremely gracious and helpful. My former student, Conrad Gempf, who was also at Tyndale at the same time, provided invaluable assistance in a number of areas. In addition, many of the Visiting Scholars and Readers at Tyndale House that year have entered into extended dialogue with me with the issues involved. Again and again I have been surprised at how many of them have also had to deal with the suicide of a relative, friend, or acquaintance. Those who have served in the pastoral ministry especially, have been quick to encourage me in this endeavor. I particularly appreciate their interaction on the chapters dealing with the theological and historical issues. They have sharpened my thinking in these areas. Needless to say, however, I take sole responsibility for the ideas expressed and the conclusions drawn.

Our book has three distinct components. The first is a series of seventeen of Gwen's poems which will give you a sense of what her thoughts and internal feelings were during the weeks and months following Kate's death. They represent a chronology of sorts in poetry, and we have used them to introduce each of the chapters of the book.

The first five chapters are a series of short pieces that tell something of the experiences of the first few weeks and months of the mourning process and some of the things we found that helped us through those difficult days. These chapters are very personal. They record what happened to us. Your own experiences, like those of the rest of our family, will certainly differ in detail, and perhaps even in broad outline, but this is the way it was with the two of us.

Next, there is a series of chapters that look at what the Bible and the church say about suicide. Many people simply assume that the church's traditional teaching is correct: suicide is a mortal sin. However, as I worked through the accounts of suicides in the Bible, I found, much to my surprise, that the Bible nowhere explicitly condemns suicide. That discovery forced me to a reexamination of the whole issue from a theological viewpoint. Chapters 6 to 12 deal with this aspect of the work.

Chapters 13 to 15, and the Epilogue return to the more personal elements of our story, dealing with some of the longer-range aspects of the grieving process.

Finally, in the Appendix, I have gathered a number of the more important passages from the writings of the ancient philosophers and the church fathers and theologians. This material is familiar to the specialists in biblical studies and church history and is easily accessible to them, but I suspect that the average person would have difficulty locating many of these sources. Most readers may want to ignore that section, but anyone who is interested in examining the background of the ideas developed in chapters 6 to 12 will find the Appendix the place to start. A short list of suggestions for further reading is added at the end.

The book is an attempt to put all of this into a form that may be of help to others—not to try to exorcise a ghost, nor to re-live the turmoil and anguish of those months—but simply to tell as best I can how we came to grips with the reality of the suicide of a woman we loved and to record some of the things we learned as we struggled to pick up the pieces of our shattered lives in the aftermath of a violent and tragic act.

—G. Lloyd Carr, September 1988

A SUICIDE REASONS

To die this once
will bring release
from smaller deaths
that never cease,
nor ever bring deliverance.

CHAPTER ONE

THE END

It was not quite cold enough to snow, as the raw December wind off the North Atlantic swept the drizzle and dull silver fog across the rows of tombstones and stunted trees and into the faces of the mourners clustered quietly on the gentle slope of the hillside.

There was no open grave, just the small gray box on a small piece of plastic grass, and a single red rose wet by the gentle rain. Only a handful of ashes and the memories of a life remained.

The minister's quiet voice rehearsed the familiar words. "Let not your hearts be troubled . . . believe in God, believe . . . in me . . . resurrection and . . . life . . . whoever believes in me . . . though he die, will live, and whoever believes in me . . . never die. Christ . . . raised from the dead . . . first fruits . . . fallen asleep . . . by man came death . . . by man . . . the resurrection of the dead . . . in Adam all die . . . in Christ . . . all be made alive . . . we believe . . . Jesus died . . . rose again . . . through Jesus, God will bring . . . those who have fallen asleep." But while our ears heard them, their very familiarity relegated the hearing to the unconscious.

The blur of words ended, and only the sobs, some quiet, some louder, mingled with the moan of the wind. Tears and rain streaked the faces. Fifty yards away near a clump of small trees, the gravediggers stood waiting as inconspicuously as they could. One by one the other mourners drifted off, the pastor speaking quietly to each as they left. Alone, I dropped the other red rose across the little casket, and through my tears whispered "Goodbye, Katie."

As I turned to join Gwen who stood a few feet away, Pastor Jim was still there. He said nothing. Instead he just reached out and embraced me, then walked slowly back with us across the wet, brown grass to where we had parked half-an-hour before. He embraced us both again, said goodbye, and moved quietly to his own car.

We sat in the car, not speaking, just watching the rain run down the windows. The gravediggers tossed their cigarettes away and started the job they were being paid to do. I watched until I could bear to watch no longer. Quickly I started the engine and headed out, automatically coping with the city traffic. We drove home, each of us lost in our own grief, reliving the last few days.

The previous Friday the sharp ring of the telephone had broken into my sleep. It was 6:00 on a dark December morning. My first thought was that this was a call from my chairman telling me school was cancelled because of heavy snow. But a glance out the window at the bare ground dispelled that idea. "Something's wrong," I concluded as I reached for the phone. "Hello."

"Dad?" It was Rob's voice.

Without waiting for an answer, he continued "Katie shot herself this morning."

My startled response shocked Gwen fully awake, knowing, without being aware she knew, what I had just heard. "Is she dead?" "Where?" "When?" The questions tumbled out, overlapping the answers, reflecting the confusion and chaos in my mind and in Rob's. I don't recall exactly what I learned in those few minutes and what we learned in the next hour as we reached their home and stood weeping and consoling each other in the front hall.

Edna St. Vincent Millay once wrote: "Life must go on, I

forget just why." The routine of meals is itself part of life and part of the mechanism of coping. Rob and Josh came home with us, and over a simple breakfast around the old kitchen table, we pieced together the story.

She had been at work the morning before, then she left about noon, ostensibly to attend class at a nearby college. She had said she would be home for supper, but an hour past the expected time she had not arrived. That was not particularly unusual as she had her own group of friends and acquaintances and frequently stayed with one or other of them, but a series of telephone calls failed to locate her. Then about 3:00 a.m. a local police officer had brought the news. She had been found dead in her car on a deserted beach in a neighboring town, a suicide note and a stolen gun beside her.

LOVERS

. . . and then you courted death,
and he became the friend
that promised when you needed one
he'd be there in the end.
When every painful pulsebeat
put living into doubt,
the last friend that you made,
you made to let you out.

CHAPTER TWO

FRIDAY

Emergency rooms, police stations and all-night diners are always open, but for most of the rest of us, business is done between 8:00 in the morning and 5:00 in the afternoon. And so beginning the process of picking up of the pieces had to wait until after breakfast. Rob had already telephoned Kate's mother, and we had called Pastor Jim, but now there were other family and friends who needed to be told.

Such calls are never easy, but they must be made. And in spite of the natural tendency to want to hide the ugly reality, the telling must be accurate. The local weekly will list a simple, bland obituary, but the city papers will not be so hesitant. And in these small towns, police-and-fire-radios and short-wave-scanners are a way of life.

At mid-morning we heard a footstep on the porch and the doorbell rang. A dear friend whom we had helped through some difficult times with her own children, came in, bringing a package of food with her.

"I heard on the police radio that something awful had happened," she began, as she reached out and hugged us both to her.

We talked briefly, but not much needed to be said. Her mere presence was a comfort.

Kate's brother Jack had gone to the hospital with Rob to

verify identification and make what arrangements were necessary with the authorities. Pastor Jim met them there for that painful time.

Then we had the trip to make through the winter morning to the police station in the distant town to collect her belongings and recover her car. The young officer behind the desk was quietly sympathetic, but not too helpful. Our business must be with the Chief, who at the moment was over at the town hall.

We walked back through the parking lot to the street, waited for a solitary car to pass, and crossed to enter the old stone and brick building whose new plate glass doors gave an incongruous flair to the quiet patina of the weathered facade and the well-worn stone steps. In the pale light of the December morning, the glass reflected our images back to us like the dark shadows that haunted our thoughts.

Inside, we found the Chief, coffee cup in hand, chatting with a couple of other men. He seemed to sense who we were, because even before we introduced ourselves he turned from his companions, quickly finished his coffee, and started toward the lobby where we were waiting.

Small talk is the safety valve to relieve the pressure of the undeveloped relationship. The weather . . . the season . . . did the Celtics win last night . . . how were the Patriots going to do against the Cowboys on Sunday . . . the traffic . . . the weather again . . . were the topics of our conversation as we left the building and crossed the still quiet street back to the police station. We discussed everything except the real reason for our presence here in this cold morning.

But business must be done, and once inside, he was all business. He told us quickly how the car had been discovered by two young people on the beach about 1:15 a.m. He described the clutter of odds and ends, the books and papers, the butts and stubs of many cigarettes, the half-empty bottle, the gun she had "borrowed" from one of her friends, and the note she had left.

But he didn't mention the tiny hole, so small it could hardly be seen, in the back of the seat, or the traces of blood still in the creases of the leather.

I collected her things. Two half-filled grocery bags from the local supermarket held them all, and as I carried them out and set them on the floor of my car, the fetid aroma of her pungent Indian perfume filled the closed space.

The Chief was angry at the accounts that had already appeared in the morning papers, but was careful about our feelings. At one point he drew me aside and asked quietly, as he watched Rob wiping off the car seat with damp paper towels: "Is the boy all right?" Then after making me a copy of the note she had left, he shook our hands formally and said, "Next time we meet, I hope it is under happier circumstances."

WHY?

*You revelled deeply
in your pain,
until, with only death
to gain,
gave one last cry
to sever hurt—
then one last fierce goodbye.*

CHAPTER THREE

SATURDAY

In spite of the promise of God's loving concern and of the Lord's return, we all, in this life, will have tribulation and sorrow. All the faith this side of heaven will not remove the reality that we are humans living in a fallen world. And, Christians though we are, we are not exempt from the fact that bad things do, in fact, happen to good people.

That means, too, that the current teaching of the "health and wealth gospel" must be resolutely seen for what it is: a serious distortion of the truth. To teach a people, or to let yourself be taught, that if only one has enough faith, one will be able to escape sorrow and trouble, is to reject the clear teaching and obvious examples of the New Testament. Both our Lord himself, as he faced the agony of Gethsemane and the torture of crucifixion, and the apostle Paul, troubled with his "thorn in the flesh," learned that God's grace was sufficient—not by deliverance from the cross or by the removal of the "thorn"—but by the empowering to endure, and the strength to get on with the task.

The Psalmist said "Thy word have I hid in mine heart, that I might not sin against thee" (119:11, KJV), and over the generations, God's people have discovered the sustaining power of the Word, not just against sin, but also as a support in time of trouble. The apostle Peter calls us to be ready always to give an answer to any who ask for a reason for our hope (1 Pet. 3:15).

These ideas need to come together for us. And if your experience is anything like mine, in times of disaster and upheaval in life, there is no time to start hunting around for passages of Scripture or for building carefully constructed theological masterpieces. What turns out to be the strongest support in these crises is what has been learned and established in the long, regular study of God's Word. The heat of the battle will test the armor, but the iron must have been forged slowly and tempered gradually over the regular routine of daily living. Otherwise, in the crisis, the shield will fail and we will be left defenseless.

The shaping of the armor and the tempering of the weapons is a long, gradual process. So too is the process of building a strong foundation in the Christian life. It cannot be done quickly, it may not be done at all, but if one is to do it, one must keep at it regularly, day by day, month by month, year by year.

Kate's family is a typically large, close, Italian Catholic one. There are a myriad of cousins, uncles, aunts, nieces, nephews, children and grandchildren, sisters, brothers, and in-laws, in a complex series of overlapping and interconnected relationships. And in spite of the Catholic belief that suicide is a mortal sin for which there is no forgiveness, the family felt it wanted at least a simple wake at the funeral parlor. So one was arranged for Saturday afternoon at two.

A few minutes after the hour I parked on the street, walked slowly up to the front door, and entered. The place was deserted, but I found the right room and crossed through the dim light and over the thick carpet to where the open coffin lay at the front of the room.

I have seen death many times: the tarpaulin-covered body at the side of the road, one bloody foot still visible, and the mangled wreckage of the cars a silent witness to disaster; the living death of dear friends in the final stages of cancer; colleagues and co-workers, young and old, whose cheery words "I'll see you tomorrow" belied the heart attacks that took them before dawn; the infant victim of crib-death and the anguished parents wrestling with the guilt of wondering if they somehow could have prevented it; the pale, limp body of the young woman caught in the current and swept off the sandbar to her death, her black bathing suit a premature shroud; powdered and painted effigies in satin-lined coffins, the make-up unable to conceal totally the violence done.

As Eve says in P. W. Turner's powerful drama *Cry Dawn in Dark Babylon*:

> Abel, Abel my son.
> So still . . . so still and alien . . .
> This then is death,
> This thing that has the mould
> And outward semblance of my son,
> But is no more my son.

I stood beside the coffin a few moments, my brain a turmoil of confusion. Grief, loss, and pity flooded over me, but the most overwhelming feeling was one of waste. For those who are desperately ill, death can be a welcome relief. Sudden death by accident or heart failure always shocks and devastates. But suicide, deliberate self-destruction, especially of a talented and gifted young person, appalls. The unfulfilled dreams, the unfinished work, the uncompleted promise, all mock like demons.

For me Kate's death was a shock, but not a surprise. She had undergone several years of professional counseling, but she still found it difficult to integrate her experience and low self-esteem with the expectations of family, church, and society. Nor did her chosen circle of friends provide much help. She had attempted suicide before, but failed. We tried to help, to encourage and care, but bit by bit she withdrew from all of us. We sensed, but could not really know, how deeply she was hurting. By mid-summer I had known instinctively it would only be a matter of when and how. From early

September, every time I went out I expected to arrive home to hear the news. Every time I saw an accident on the highway, my heart skipped until, relieved, I saw it was not a small blue car involved.

Crossing to the back of the room, I found a chair in one corner, and sat down. A moment later, Kate's older brother Sam came out of the office area, chatted briefly, and said "Lloyd, I want you to say something to the family when they all get here."

I felt in no condition to try to comfort others. But he was insistent. I borrowed a Bible from the undertaker and turned to Paul's words in 1 Thessalonians 4:13-18. It was a familiar passage, memorized years ago, but one which I had not looked at for some time. Now in the quiet hush of the dimly lit room, I read again those familiar words:

> But we would not have you ignorant, brethren, concerning those who are asleep, that you may not grieve as others do who have no hope. For since we believe that Jesus died and rose again, even so, through Jesus, God will bring with him those that have fallen asleep. For this we declare to you by the word of the Lord, that we who are alive, who are left until the coming of the Lord, shall not precede those who have fallen asleep. For the Lord himself will descend from heaven with a cry of command, and with the archangel's call, and with the sound of the trumpet of God. And the dead in Christ will rise first; then we who are alive, who are left, shall be caught up together with them in the clouds to meet the Lord in the air; and so we shall always be with the Lord. Therefore comfort one another with these words.

Two lines from the passage stood out: the one which had first come to my mind as I began to respond to Sam's request, "that you may not grieve as others do who have no hope"; and on the re-reading, "comfort one another with these words." The word for me in this situation was the latter. And I personalized it. "Comfort them with these words."

"What words?" I thought. "What can I say? I can scarcely think clearly. I am certain I cannot control my tears in private, let alone try to speak publicly. Lord, why me?" And then the words of the apostle Peter came to my mind. "Always be prepared to make a defense . . . for the hope that is in you." I looked back at the passage, and a simple outline began to form in my thinking.

I saw that the text does not say "don't grieve." It does say "don't grieve as others do who have no hope." Of course we grieve. Death is ugly, and our loss is real. The whole course of human history bears witness to the reality of separation. The closed coffin and the raw scar in the ground mark the finality we each must face, for ourselves and for each of our loved ones. Their going forces us to deal with the certainty of our own departure, and our grieving for them is in part a grieving for ourselves. Death is part of life, and of course we grieve.

The difference for the Christian is "the hope." Tied here explicitly to the reality of the death *and resurrection* of Christ (1 Thess. 4:14), is the certainty of our Lord's return, himself triumphant over death, and in his coming, our triumph too. The last enemy is defeated, and the reunion is assured.

It was clear now what I had to say: nothing fancy, no elaborate sermon, just a simple sharing of what I knew Kate's faith to have been. I could talk of her depression and despair, of the turmoil of her life in the last months, but I could talk, too, of her allegiance to Christ which remained, even in her suicide note. She could not cope with life and in despair threw herself on the mercy of Christ. I could not condone the action, but I could understand. I could talk about the simplicity of the gospel and the grace we shared. I could allay the horror the Catholic teaching invokes by a simple affirmation of Jesus' words.

> My sheep hear my voice, and I know them, and they
> follow me; and I give them eternal life, and they shall
> never perish, and no one shall snatch them out of my
> hand. My Father who has given them to me is greater
> than all, and no one is able to snatch them out of my
> Father's hand (John 10:27-29).

And I could share as simply as I knew how, the truth of the gospel: of forgiveness freely offered through Christ.

And so it was that, standing to one side of the open coffin, I read the words of Paul and shared the thoughts that had shaped themselves in my mind. It was not easy. I could not control my tears, and several times my voice broke and I had to pause. But in sharing the simplicity of the gospel, I knew the Lord's presence and his sustaining power.

That simple talk was the most difficult thing I have ever done, but in attempting to comfort others, I found again the truth of Jesus' word "My grace is sufficient."

A YOUNG SUICIDE

You picked your way
to the other side,
where those who tire of living
hide.
And the bridge you crossed
so instantly,
left spans of sorrow here
for me.

Must I pick my way
across this world
day after day, after meager day?

CHAPTER FOUR

SUNDAY

Friday and Saturday had been cool and damp, with raw, daytime temperatures hovering just above freezing. But the New England weather changes rapidly, and Sunday morning dawned clear and bright, but bitterly cold. The northwest gale that had cleared the heavy clouds brought no snow, just frigid winds that chilled the body but could not affect our already numbed spirits.

There seemed to be no compelling incentive to shower and shave and leave the warm anonymity of the house to endure the below-zero temperatures and gale winds for the short drive through the winter morning to church. Why bother? Who can concentrate on worship or on God when the whole world seems to have collapsed around you? All we wanted to do was hide from prying eyes and intrusive questions, to crawl deeper into our hole and lick our wounds.

I was relieved I had no responsibilities in church that morning. My adult Bible class had concluded the week before Thanksgiving, and my teaching responsibilities in the new quarter would not begin until the second Sunday of the New Year. Nor was it my turn to assist on the platform for the worship. Why not just stay in bed?

But we are social creatures as much as private creatures, and there was a deep, almost unconscious awareness that even if we didn't feel like worship and fellowship, we needed to be with God's people. We arrived a few minutes early.

This had been our church home for over twenty years. These were the people who had welcomed us when we were strangers to the community, one more "student family" who they (and we), thought would be here today, then in three or four years graduate, and move on, severing all contact with the congregation. But we had stayed. I had completed my graduate degrees and returned to teach in my old college. We had built friendships and put down roots. These were our people. We had laughed together, and worked together, and worshiped together, and mourned together many times. But now for us, it was a different mood and a vastly changed situation.

There was a sense of hesitancy on our part as well as theirs. What does one say in the face of suicide? Does one say anything at all? The loss, shame, and desolation crowd in on all of us, and there is the hopeless sense of our inability to cope with it all.

After the first awkward moments as we came into the entrance hall, there had been the usual condolences of the people there. Then more embarrassed silence until, at the foot of the stairs to the sanctuary, a couple whose adopted son had taken his own life a few years before met us. She embraced Gwen; he grasped my hand. I sensed the tears in his eyes and voice as he squeezed my hand and said quietly "We understand . . . we've been there."

The sanctuary was already well filled, but we found seats near the back. A part of the congregation was the usual, transient, student population, and there were a few other visitors, but it was one of those in-between Sundays. Thanksgiving was two weeks past. Christmas was still two weeks away, and most of those present were old friends and familiar faces.

The organist had begun the prelude, and the congregation was settling into worship. I have absolutely no recollection of any of the service except Pastor Jim's announcement of the

afternoon memorial service in the cemetery chapel. Apart
from that, the morning was a blur of sound and movement
that somehow in its very confusion, began to order our internal chaos. Finally we were conscious that the benediction
was over and the postlude had begun. We had the task of facing others again.

At the back of the church, some were hesitant, holding
back, unsure of what to do or say. But others were not. Our
associate pastor, a vibrant young man the same age as our
son, came across, put his arms around both of us, and said
simply "I'm glad you're here." And then the hugs and tears,
as our friends gathered around and enfolded us in their love
and concern. Our loss was their loss as well, and their condolences revealed their sorrow. "When one of the body
hurts, we all hurt," one dear friend reminded us. And we
knew they knew.

It had been a trying morning. We had been reluctant to
face the church family, but knew we must. One friend, put it
this way: "I was overwhelmed when I saw you come in
before the service. I sat back here and cried for you. But this
was the right place to come today, and the Lord will bless
you for it." At the time we couldn't understand, but looking
back, our decision to meet with God's people for worship, to
be near our friends on that first Sunday morning, was the
beginning of the healing. We need each other.

UNPOSSESSED

You were never mine
to keep.

Letting go is hard
for this possessive heart.
I weep
at the releasing,
at having nothing left to hold,
forgetting when I grasp
that all that is
is given
not for keeps but loaned.

CHAPTER FIVE

PICKING UP THE PIECES

I f your calendar is anything like ours, the weeks between Thanksgiving and Christmas are crammed full. The Advent season, at least for us, is a time of celebration, fellowship, and preparation for the day of remembering our Lord's birth. And if there are children or grandchildren around, there is the added excitement of toys and candy and Christmas stockings. The multitude of plans and decisions about which events to participate in have been settled weeks before and preparations made. And then suddenly death barged in.

The first three or four days are chaotic. Everything else takes second place to the immediate need to "make arrangements." Someone must deal with the funeral director, the cemetery officials, the minister, the hospital, and in the case of suicide, the police and other authorities. Special friends and relatives who live at a distance need to be notified. The tasks which must be done, are done, but everything else is shunted aside before the pressing immediacy of death.

By Wednesday noon the graveside service was over. Friends and family had gone their separate ways back to the responsibilities of the day or to the empty desolation of grief. Suddenly there was nothing more that "had to be done," and the gray, empty days closed in.

The annual Christmas dinner for the families and staff of

the college was set for Friday evening. For many of us, it is one of the social highlights of the school year. We had sent our reservations in weeks before, and the date was marked on our calendars. But this was only a week after Katie's death. Should we attend? Our impulse was to say "no"—we were in mourning and celebration seemed sacrilegious. But by Friday we knew we had to go. It was not the celebration we needed. "Celebration" was neither repugnant nor attractive, but irrelevant. What we needed was to be with our friends. We needed their support and their comfort. We needed to be reassured that they cared about us. There was nothing they could do to cancel the reality and horror of the last eight days, but their strength and their love and concern would be shared with us. We knew that. We went.

In December on the east coast the sun sets early. We left the house a little before 6:00 p.m., but it had already been dark nearly an hour. The festive mood of the dining hall, sharpened by the beautifully set tables and the lighted candles, formed a stark contrast to our own inner feelings. Already many of the tables were full, but we found a place and joined the circle that included several friends of long standing. We entered into the spirit of the evening as best we could, and to our surprise, found that we, too, could enjoy the celebration.

We discovered anew the real significance of the Christmas season—to celebrate the coming to earth of God himself. The incarnation was God's way of starting the process of *his* dealing with the fact of death in his creation and his way of affirming that he was willing to face all that human beings face—even death itself—to give hope to the hopeless. Not without reason, we realized, was this called the *Advent* season. The *coming* of the Prince of Peace marked the beginning of new beginnings. There was still much sorrow, many tears, our own and those of our friends, but we could cry together, joined by a common faith in God's real involvement with us in our common grief.

And there were still many other things that called us back to the world of the living. Several weeks earlier, we had agreed to make a pre-Christmas trip to Boston to attend a recital given by a friend of a friend. It would have been easy to beg off, since we really didn't know the woman who was to sing, but our friend had been very close to Kate, and for her sake we went.

The recital hall was just behind the Cambridge Common off Harvard Square. It is an area where it is almost impossible to find on-street parking, so I dropped the others off at the hall, then went to search for a parking place. I found one only three blocks away, parked and locked the car, and then, alone and with my mind in turmoil, walked back along the dark, wet streets to join Gwen and our friends waiting in the warmth and brightness of the foyer.

In spite of our mutual sorrow and grieving, our expectations for the evening were high. We were not disappointed. The soloist was a lyric soprano, trained in opera at the conservatory, and already making a name for herself in the professional world. But she had come into a relationship with Jesus Christ, and was also using her talent in the choir of the church our friends attended. The evening's program was varied. Some shorter and longer pieces from the standard repertoire displayed the beauty and range of her strong soprano. But it was the simplicity of the old story of Christ's coming told through the music of some of the great masters and presented in the sweet and glorious sounds of her magnificent voice that drew us back again to wonder at God's grace toward his people and to praise him even in sorrow.

There was the daily routine of living. There were letters and cards to answer, telephone calls to return, shopping to be done, groceries to get, and then the trip home for Christmas. We both have family and friends still living in Toronto, and in late summer we had planned the Christmas visit, little knowing how different the circumstances would be in December.

By 6:00 a.m. we were on the road, just early enough to be ahead of the Boston-bound morning commuters. A little before seven we had picked up our toll ticket and were heading west along the Massachusetts Turnpike through the pale gray dawn.

After Worcester and the Route 15 turnoff to Hartford and New York City, the traffic thinned to only an occasional truck. The highway, threading through the snowy Berkshire hills, stark and cold in the morning sun, wound down into New York state and across the Hudson. The wind sweeping down the bleak river valley moaned through the steel girders of the bridge, echoing the silent moaning in our hearts. From Albany, past Utica along the banks of the snow-covered, frozen Mohawk River, we were stirred again by the beauty of the creation, but after Syracuse the miles of empty farmland, scarcely interesting even in good times, seemed to drag us down to their own flat dreariness.

It was nearly dark again by the time we left the throughway and turned north towards Niagara. With the fading light and falling temperatures, it had started to snow, and the heavy rush hour traffic on the bypass through Tonawanda claimed my full attention until we reached the Grand Island toll booth. Off the island I had the choice of the highway and the bypass to the bridge at Queenston, or the quieter Parkway past the power plant intake and the backside of the chemical factories to the Rainbow Bridge just below the Falls. Even though it meant a bit more city traffic, I chose the latter where the Christmas lights glistened against the snow-covered streets as we moved slowly with the holiday crowds. Then across the bridge, its intricate steelwork filigreed with ice from the mist of the falls, through the customs checkpoint, we turned right through the city onto the Queen Elizabeth Way and the last eighty miles to home.

From the Welland Canal bridge at St. Catharines all the way to Toronto, much of the farmland is gone, and the highway is flanked with residential areas clustered among the thousands of commercial offices and industrial buildings. And now, after dark, the lighted Christmas trees in countless living rooms and the sometimes beautiful, sometimes garish juxtaposition of the Christmas decorations with the multitude of advertising signs merged into a constant ribbon of colored light hedging the speeding traffic. The orange-red glow from the steel mills reflected in the choppy waters of Hamilton harbor, and from the high arch of the Burlington Bridge seemed to reveal an eerie sunken city whose ghostly lights still celebrated the holiday. Our conversation, which had been curtailed in the heavy confusion before the border, surged again, then ebbed, as we turned up Highway 10, through the city traffic past Dundas Street and under the railway tracks, until after the last traffic light and the last corner, we were in the parking lot and home.

But now it all had to be retold, not just once, but over and over again to parents, siblings, aunts, uncles, cousins, friends—all who needed to know or wanted to hear what had "gone wrong"—how "it" had happened. In living rooms, kitchens, dens—all the places our friends and families lived—we recounted the events, told what we knew, and relived the tragedy.

And then back home the telling continued. For our part, we found it helpful just to be able to talk about the whole situation. It was our great privilege to find friends who were willing to hear us out, not because they had to be told, but who simply recognized that *for us* it was important to have someone who was just willing to listen.

Well into the late winter Gwen met with her friends, one at a time, and over lunch in the sometimes dull, sometimes bright kitchen, talked and shared together about the part that Kate had played in their lives. It was not judgmental or morbid curiosity that motivated the questioning. It was concern to understand, and by understanding, comfort. And with each retelling, as difficult as each was, we sensed an easing of the pain. The very telling itself peeled back another layer of sorrow.

THE WAY IT IS

Encountering death,
(that final phase)
I notice no returning.
The fallen sparrow's swift decay disturbs,
and in the crematorium
one I loved submits to her bright burning.
And many homeless, sick and maimed
contend for death, and find their way
before the spring,
before the snowdrop's wakening.

CHAPTER SIX

A LOOK AT SOME BIBLE STORIES

Suicide is an ugly word, and the deed is an ugly deed. And in the Christian community, particularly among evangelicals, the common idea is that real Christians don't commit suicide. However, the sad reality is that real Christians sometimes do, and Christian families have to deal with the shame and guilt, as well as the grief and sense of loss and betrayal that suicide brings.

But beyond this, one of the most distressing things about facing the suicide of a friend or loved one is not the mere finality of the act, nor the devastation of the loss, but the belief that somehow suicide is a very great sin. The Catholic community, traditionally, has looked upon it as a mortal sin, beyond forgiveness. The official position of the Roman Catholic Church is still that if deliberate, "suicide is intrinsically evil . . . and no circumstances can ever justify it."[1] Because it is "self-murder" that allows no time for penance and confession before death, it is a "mortal" sin for which there is no forgiveness.

Most of us within the protestant tradition would not go quite so far as our Catholic friends, but would probably agree essentially with the position taken a few years ago in a report by a special commission on suicide appointed by the Archbishop of Canterbury. "It is generally accepted by all who hold the Christian faith that suicide is a sin. Most non-Christians, although not regarding it as a sin against the deity, nevertheless tend to consider it to be undesirable, and in many cases, an anti-social act."

And as if the wounds were not deep enough, we have the nagging sense that *perhaps* the Catholic Church's teaching is right after all—that our dead loved one is consigned to an eternity of separation from God—the unforgivable sin has been committed, and there is no hope. Whether or not we are consciously aware of this attitude, it is such an ingrained element in much Christian thinking that it seriously complicates our ability to come to grips with the reality of the situation.

In the first few weeks after Kate's death I found myself relying quite simply on the promises that had sustained me through those first days. Then as time passed and I gradually worked through my grief, I began to wonder about the whole issue. I knew the Catholic Church's teaching that suicide was unforgivable because there was no opportunity for penance. But that idea did not square with my understanding that Christ's sacrifice was sufficient to cover *all* sin. And I remembered a part of Kate's last note where in the depths of her despair and depression, she had written "All I can ask is Christ's forgiveness and understanding. . . . I feel sick, sick at heart and tired of living. . . . [I] pray that Jesus will take me." Kate *had* asked for forgiveness. And I wondered how many other suicides had done the same thing. There is time in that eternal moment to ask—and there *is* God's grace.

I long ago learned that experience teaches much, but I also learned long ago that any one person's experience is very limited. And so I turned, as I had so many times before, to the Bible and then to the library and the collected experiences of our predecessors and peers to try to discover an answer to my wonderings. As I read and studied the material, I found some surprising things.

I had assumed the common ideas mentioned above were in fact well-established positions that had some biblical foundation. But to my surprise, I discovered that this was not the case. And with that discovery I knew that this book would have to be more than just a telling of our story. It would have to include a careful look at some of the key writings of early church fathers and of the biblical material itself.

It may seem as if these next few chapters are an unimportant interruption in the story, but in fact, they provide a most crucial perspective for dealing with the question of suicide.

There are a number of places where Scripture speaks directly to this issue. The biblical instance that probably comes to mind first is that of Judas Iscariot who betrayed Jesus to the Jewish authorities and then took his own life. We will return to Judas shortly, but first let us examine the other biblical accounts of suicide.

In the Old Testament there are four clear cases of suicide, one instance of what is really revenge killing in which the avenger dies along with those whom he destroys, and one case which may be seen as euthanasia or "mercy killing," but which is usually considered a suicide.

To begin with the last mentioned, we turn to the story of Abimelech in Judges 9. Abimelech is one of those strange characters who appears on the scene during the tumultuous years of the Hebrew settlement in the land of Canaan. He was the son of the great hero and judge, Gideon, and a concubine from Shechem. After his father's death, Abimelech, with the support of the citizens of Shechem, staged a military coup. During the course of action he murdered seventy of his brothers—sons of Gideon—and declared himself to be king. For three years he was able to rule the small circle of territory in the northern Samaritan highlands around Shechem. He was a petty king with a petty kingdom.

But our interest in Abimelech is not his birth or his life or his kingship, but his death. It was in a military campaign against the fortified city of Thebez (Tirzeh) that he met his end. During the siege of the city, the army mounted an assault upon the strong tower where the men and women of the city had taken refuge. Abimelech's strategy was to burn the tower as he had done earlier in the conquest of Shechem. This time, however, as he approached the door, one of the women of the city threw a small millstone from the top of the tower, and hit Abimelech on the head, crushing his skull. "Then [Abimelech] called hastily to the young man his armor-bearer and said to him, 'Draw your sword and kill me, lest men say of me, "A woman killed him."' And his young man thrust him through, and he died" (Judg. 9:54).

Abimelech's death, since it was not self-inflicted is not, strictly speaking, a suicide. But it is probable that if the armor-bearer, had not obeyed his master's command, Abimelech would have found some other person to carry out his order. His was a borderline case. The blow was struck by another, but the order was given by the victim.

Where Abimelech is a largely unknown character, there is another judge who is perhaps one of the best known characters in the Old Testament. We speak, of course, of Samson. Who, in the western world, at least, has not heard of the episode of Samson and Delilah? Whether through story, music, opera, movies, or late-night television reruns, the image of the seduction, betrayal, and ultimate destruction of the hero as he brings the Philistine temple crashing down upon the assembled worshipers, is common coin.

This is a strange story. Foolish Samson, falling for Delilah's wiles, humiliated, blinded, and shackled, is set to animal-work, turning the great millstone in the Gaza prison. But our interest in Samson is not in his liaison with Delilah, nor even with the details of his betrayal and captivity. Again, our concern is with his death.

Judges 16:23-31 records the story. The blinded captive is brought before the assembled dignitaries and the crowd of onlookers to be the object of their ridicule and taunts. At last he persuades the boy who is leading him to let him rest between the pillars supporting the roof of the temple.

Standing there he prays "Remember me, O Lord God, remember me: give me strength only this once, O God, and let me at one stroke be avenged on the Philistines for my two eyes. . . . Let me die with the Philistines" (Judg. 16:28-30, NEB). In one final feat of strength he "bowed with all his might" (v. 30, RSV) against the pillars of the temple and perished with his Philistine tormenters. Revenge and self-destruction combine in a single bloody act.

Turning to cases of actual suicide in the Old Testament, we begin with two other characters, Ahithophel and Zimri, who are equally as unfamiliar as Abimelech.

Ahithophel had been one of King David's chief advisors and most respected counselors (2 Sam. 16:23). But when David's son Absalom revolted against his father and declared himself king in David's place, Ahithophel abandoned David and joined forces with the rebels. As counselor to the new king, Ahithophel proposed a military strategy that would have sealed David's fate and ensured the succession of Absalom. But his counsel was rejected "so that the Lord might bring evil upon Absalom" (2 Sam. 17:14), and the advice of a less wise counselor, Hushai, was accepted.

Ahithophel's end was quick and definite. "When Ahithophel saw that his counsel was not followed, he saddled his ass, and went off home to his own city. And he set his house in order, and hanged himself; and he died, and was buried in the tomb of his father" (2 Sam. 17:23).

His action may seem precipitous, but Ahithophel knew that he had made a fatal miscalculation. He had sided with what he now knew to be the losing faction, and his life was in jeopardy. He recognized that execution as a traitor was inevitable, and so rather than wait, putting his whole family in jeopardy, he "set his house in order," then anticipating the ultimate victory of his former sovereign, took his own life, a forfeit for guilt that could not be made good.

The brief, violent, and bloody reign of King Zimri of Israel also ended in suicide. Under the twenty-four-year reign of Baasha (1 Kings 15:33–16:7), the Northern Kingdom extended its frontiers and international influence. But it also continued in the idolatrous and degraded worship of the Baal cult which King Jeroboam had introduced (1 Kings 12:25-33; 13:33-34; 14:7-16).

The Israelite kingdom was open to military aggression from two directions: the northern frontier faced the forces of Phoenicia and Syria (Aram/Damascus) and in the south, Judah and the remnants of the Philistine power along the coastal plain were a constant threat (1 Kings 15:16-22). To meet this danger on two fronts, Baasha had divided his army into two major units. The Judah-Philistine threat was held in check by the southern division under the leadership of Omri and the second division, commanded by Zimri, guarded the northern frontier.

At Baasha's death, his son Elah succeeded to the throne, and the affairs of the kingdom began to fall into disarray, as the political and social structure started to disintegrate. Elah, apparently, was a weak leader and a poor king, and within two years, Zimri launched a military coup against his monarch. During a drunken party, Zimri assassinated Elah and claimed the throne for himself. Then followed a bloody purge of the royal supporters. Zimri "killed all of the house of Baasha; he did not leave him a single male of his kinsmen or his friends" (1 Kings 16:11).

The news of the revolt and bloodbath traveled quickly. Within a couple of days, the soldiers of the southern division had declared their commander Omri to be the rightful successor to the murdered king. They marched back north and besieged Zimri in the capital city of Tirzah. The end was quick. "And when Zimri saw that the city was taken, he went into the citadel of the king's house, and burned the king's house over him with fire, and died" (1 Kings 16:18).

His coup had failed. The bloodbath he had inaugurated alienated both the army and the people. He was a traitor and a regicide, himself marked for destruction, and like Samson, deliberately chose to die in the shattered ruins. He had reigned seven days.

Next to Samson's, the best-known story of suicide in the Old Testament is that of King Saul and his armor-bearer. Saul's reign had begun auspiciously. The new king, tall, with a winsome personality and a quick mind, had also been touched in a special way by God's spirit and power (1 Sam. 9:2; 10:1, 10). Under his leadership, the Hebrews succeeded in establishing a strong, unified resistance to the Philistines and other hostile neighbors, gradually winning control of most of the territory of Palestine (1 Sam. 13–14). Eventually, however, troubled by emotional, mental, and spiritual problems, devoured by an insane jealousy toward his rival David, and beset by the reviving power of the Philistine coalition, his rule collapsed. He had reigned for over twenty years, but the end was sudden.

With the prophet Samuel, his counselor and patron, dead, his jealousy of David a consuming passion, and his own emotional and religious life a shambles, Saul saw his beloved land falling once again under the control of the Philistines. In one last, desperate effort to repulse the enemy, his army fought a brave but unsuccessful rearguard action. It was all in vain. Finally, on the heights of Mount Gilboa, overlooking the fertile Jezreel Valley, the rout was completed. The army was destroyed, and Saul's three sons were among the slain. The king himself did not escape. Pursued and badly wounded by the Philistine archers, he fell. The narrator of 1 Samuel describes the end.

> Then Saul said to his armor-bearer, "Draw your sword and thrust me through with it, lest these uncircumcised [Philistines] come and thrust me through and make sport of me." But his armor-bearer would not; for he feared greatly. Therefore Saul took his own sword and fell upon it (1 Sam. 31:4).

Like Abimilech, he preferred to die at once, honorably, than to survive for a few more hours and then die abjectly.

The armor-bearer is the overlooked participant in this episode. His "fear" was probably not fear of his king's wrath, but more likely his "awe" at the fact of his kingship. Such was his affection and respect for his master, he could not raise his hand against him even to obey a direct command. As he watched in anguish, his sovereign, respecting his loyalty and devotion, did not repeat the order, but took the fatal step himself. When the lad, heartsick, betrayed, surrounded by the fallen men of Israel, and perhaps himself also wounded "saw that Saul was dead, he also fell upon his sword, and died with him. Thus Saul died, and his three sons, and his armor-bearer, and all his men on the same day together" (1 Sam. 31:5-6).

The horror of the day and the slaughter of the Israelite army culminated in the double suicide of monarch and servant. Saul, like Samson before him, chose a quick and honorable death—even if self-inflicted—rather than submit to cruel and degrading mockery at the hands of the pagan Philistines. But even the Philistines seem to have overlooked the boy.

> On the morrow, when the Philistines came to strip the slain, they found Saul and his three sons fallen on Mount Gilboa. And they cut off his head, and stripped off his armor, and sent messengers throughout the land of the Philistines, to carry the good news to their idols and to the people. They put his armor in the temple of Ashtaroth; and they fastened his body to the wall of Beth-shan (1 Sam. 31:8-10).

One other instance of suicide is recorded in the extra-canonical book of 2 Maccabees 14:37-46.[2] During the long confrontation between the Jews and the Seleucid Greeks in the 160s B.C., Razis, one of the Jerusalem senators who had been honored by the Jews as a loyal supporter of the Jewish cause, was singled out by the Seleucid commander Nicanor for arrest. The contingent of soldiers sent to arrest Razis put the tower where he had taken refuge under siege and set fire to it. At that point, Razis, knowing all was lost, "turned his sword on himself. He preferred to die nobly rather than to fall into the hands of criminals and be subjected to gross humiliation" (14:41-42). His first attempt to kill himself was unsuccessful, so he then threw himself off the wall of the tower. Badly injured, but still alive he then ran through the crowd, climbed up on a large rock and proceeded to disembowel himself, flinging his intestines at the crowd, and finally died, "invoking the Lord of life and death to give these entrails back to him" in the resurrection.

The thirteenth-century theologian Thomas Aquinas speaks of this episode negatively, declaring that Razis killed himself "thinking to act from fortitude, yet it is not fortitude, but rather a weakness of the soul unable to bear penal evils."[3] "Penal evils" suggests that Nicanor was correct in imposing the death sentence on Razis, but there is nothing in the text of Maccabees that gives that idea. In the account, Razis is seen as a hero, willing to die rather than submit to the heathen power.

The New Testament records only one suicide—that of Judas Iscariot who betrayed Jesus, but there are two or three other accounts where suicide was perhaps the option before the individual.

Perhaps the most surprising is the episode in Jesus' life recorded in John 8:21-30. In one of his many confrontations with the Jewish religious leaders Jesus, speaking of his return to the Father, said to them "I go away, and you will seek me and die in your sin; where I am going you cannot come" (v. 21). The response of the Jews is quick and concise, and their question reveals the way they understood the comment— "Will he kill himself?" There is no horror or revulsion in their comment, only surprise. He did speak of his coming death—the life he would lay down for the forgiveness of sins (John 10:17-18)—but also a life these Jewish leaders would be responsible for taking.

A second "suicide" episode in the New Testament is recorded in Acts 16:27. Paul and Silas, in prison in Philippi on account of their missionary activities, were singing and praying through the night. About midnight there was a great earthquake that opened the doors of the prison. The jailer, thinking that his prisoners had escaped, and therefore that his own life was forfeit, drew his sword and was about to kill himself. Paul intervened to assure him that all the prisoners were still there, and that there was no need for the jailer to take his life. The jailer's instinctive reaction reveals the mind of a well-trained soldier willing to face a quick and sure death by his own hand rather than face disgrace, shame, and ultimate execution for negligence of duty.

The third of these cases is found in Paul's letter to the Philippians. This is one of the letters that Paul wrote while he was imprisoned in Rome. Although he knew it was quite possible he would be executed, his hope was that his case would be decided in his favor, and he would be released to continue his missionary activities. In verses 19-26 of the first chapter he expresses his ambivalence:

> Yes, and I shall rejoice. For I know that through your prayers and the help of the Spirit of Jesus Christ this will turn out for my deliverance, as it is my eager expectation and hope that I shall not be at all ashamed, but that with full courage now as always Christ will be honored in my body, whether by life or by death. For to me to live is Christ, and to die is gain. If it is to be life in the flesh, that means fruitful labor for me. Yet which I shall choose I cannot tell. I am hard pressed between the two. My desire is to depart and be with Christ, for that is far better. But to remain in the flesh is more necessary on your account. Convinced of this, I know that I shall remain and continue with you all, for

> your progress and joy in the faith, so that in me you
> may have ample cause to glory in Christ Jesus, because
> of my coming to you again.

It is evident, of course that the issue here is not really suicide. Paul's life could have been taken by the authorities, but there is no indication in this passage that he is contemplating suicide. Yet there is here the strong statement of the "desire" to depart this life. Many of the expressions Paul uses in this passage are also found in the writings of the Stoic philosophers in their discussions of suicide. And Paul's comment "which I shall *choose* I cannot tell," suggests that he believes that there is a choice. What holds him back is not the fear of death, nor the abhorrence of the thought of suicide, but rather the concern that for the sake of the Philippians he should remain alive for more fruitful labor.

The case of Judas is in some ways much more simple to deal with. The disciple, who according to some scholars was probably originally one of the inner circle closest to Jesus (he was, after all, the treasurer of the group, even though he was a dishonest one; John 12:6), for whatever reason, betrayed his Lord to the religious and political authorities. Whether he expected Jesus to perform some miracle and escape his captors, or whether he thought he could pressure Jesus to declare himself the Messiah and thus start the long hoped-for revolution against Rome, we shall never know for sure. What we do know is that Judas, when he saw Jesus condemned, was conscience-stricken, tried to return the money he had received for his act of betrayal, and then went out to his own death. This is not the place to attempt to solve the difficulties surrounding the records in Matthew 27:3-10 and Acts 1:18-19, or the fanciful accounts recorded in the church fathers of the second and third centuries. All that needs to be said is that Judas, the betrayer, died "remorseful" (*metamé lomai*, "change the mind"), not "repentant" (*metá noia*, "change one's actions").

There was no external threat, no civil judge pronouncing sentence. Judas judged himself, and proceeded to his own self-inflicted execution. But there is no evidence in the text of Scripture of Judas's total despair or his sense of abandonment by God. These themes appear only in the later accounts. Neither Matthew nor Luke (in Acts) shows any hint of condemning the suicide itself. The disapproved act is the betrayal, not the manner of death of the betrayer.

CREMATED

This fine ash
leaves no spark,
gives no warmth,
saves nothing for me
to remember.
If I could fan it
to life,
fire would leap
like burnished September.

CHAPTER SEVEN

SOME OBSERVATIONS

It usually comes as a surprise to discover that there are so many instances of suicide recorded in the Bible. It is usually even more of a surprise to discover how these episodes are treated by the biblical authors. More than 1,200 years separate the earliest (Abimelech) about 1100-1200 B.C. from the latest (the Philippian jailer) sometime in the early 50s of the first century A.D. Yet the response is consistent across the centuries. And in looking at this series of biblical episodes of suicide, three common elements emerge:

1. The suicides follow some military defeat or other terrible humiliation that indicates death or torture is inevitable. In these contexts, suicide is seen as "death with honor."

In the case of Abimelech, his request for death was simply to hurry what was already inevitable. He had been mortally wounded by a blow to the head administered by a woman. His options seemed to him to be to die honorably and quickly by the sword, or abjectly "at the hand of a woman" in a few minutes or hours. He chose the former, but the ignominy remained. One hundred fifty years later, in King David's time, Abimelech is still the butt of ridicule and disrespect. In the report of the death of Uriah the Hittite, the husband of Bathsheba with whom David had committed adultery, David is asked "Who killed Abimelech. . . ? Did not a woman cast an upper millstone upon him from the wall, so that he died at Thebez?" (2 Sam. 11:21).

Samson's death, too, although it is linked with an act of revenge upon Israel's enemies, is still self-inflicted in the face of torment beyond bearing. The ancient Jewish historian Josephus, who lived about the same time as Jesus, has this to say of Samson: "It is but right to admire the man for his valor, his strength, and the grandeur of his end, as also for the wrath which he cherished to the last against his enemies."[1]

It is important to note in this context that Samson's prayer is two-fold: (1) for strength to take revenge on the Philistines, and (2) to die. And God answers both prayers. Here is a self-willed death carried out, if not with divine approval, at the very least with divine help without which he would have been unable to complete the task.

Similarly, for both Ahithophel and Zimri, different though their circumstances were, there was the dual despair of having backed an unsuccessful revolution and the resultant threat of ignominious death at the hands of the victors. Because of all of this, life with honor was now impossible; death with honor was not. Suicide provided the option. Zimri's bloodthirsty vengeance on the family and friends of Baasha following the coup was brought to a fitting climax by the conflagration in the royal house and his own death in the burning ruins.

Ahithophel's action, while equally fatal, seems to have been motivated by a concern to make sure his family did not suffer unduly for his errors. He did not destroy himself in the shadow of the capital city in a fit of frustration and hurt feeling. Rather he took care to return to his home, made sure all his affairs were satisfactorily arranged, and only then took his life. Had he waited the inevitable return of the victorious David, he would have been executed as a traitor, his family disgraced, and his property confiscated. But by his own action he forestalled that eventuality, and provided for his family's future security.

2. The suicide is treated by the author/narrator, as well as by the rest of the people in the account, as simply another death. There is no evidence of desecration, abandonment, or lack of care for the bodies of the suicides. In cases where burial is mentioned, the burial is in the family tomb if possible, otherwise in some other designated place.

It is important to note the response of those who cared for the dead. Although there is no direct scriptural evidence for the burial of Abimelech, Zimri, or Saul's armor-bearer, neither is there any evidence that their bodies were desecrated or left unburied. In the case of Judas, the betrayer, the assumption is that he was buried in "The Field of Blood"—the field which had been purchased with the "blood money" he had received for betraying Jesus—and which later was used as a burial ground for "strangers" (aliens and others) who had no family tomb in Jerusalem (Matt. 27:6-8).

But in the other instances, there is unambiguous evidence. Samson's brothers and family retrieved his shattered body from the ruins of the Gaza temple and carried it forty miles to bury it in the tomb of their father Manoah (Judg. 16:31). And even though he died a suicide, Samson is included by the author of the book of Hebrews in the New Testament in the list of heroes of the faith (Heb. 11:32) who "of old, received divine approval" (Heb. 11:2).

Ahithophel, too, was buried in his father's tomb. There was no disgrace attached to family as a result, for Ahithophel's son Eliam later appears as one of David's mighty men of valor (2 Sam. 23:34).

Saul's case is somewhat different. Gibea, his family home, was probably under Philistine control at the time of his death. He was in a real sense, an exile and a stranger; fallen far from home. His Philistine adversaries mutilated his body, cutting off his head and (probably) sending it back with his captured armor to the temple of their goddess. Then in a final act of mockery, they fastened his headless body and the bodies of his three sons to the city wall of Bethshan—a grisly example of the fate of those who dare oppose the Philistines and their great goddess Asherah.

But Saul still had some devout and loyal allies:

> When the inhabitants of Jabesh-gilead heard what the Philistines had done to Saul, all the valiant men arose, and went all night, and took the body of Saul and the bodies of his sons from the wall of Beth-shan; and they came to Jabesh and burnt them there. And they took their bones and buried them under the tamarisk tree in Jabesh, and fasted seven days (1 Sam. 31:11-13).

They could not prevent the spectacle, but at the risk of their own lives, they did what they could to give the fallen king and his princely sons proper burial in the place of honor in their city. And they mourned for seven days.

3. Thirdly, the texts are unanimous in that they give no indication that suicide is in any sense a sin. There is not a single case of condemnation for the act itself. The suicide is treated by the author/narrator, as well as by the rest of the people in the account as simply another death.

An interesting comment on this idea is found in the Rabbinic literature. In both the *Mishna* and the *Talmud*, the most important religious books for the Jews after the Old Testament itself, there is the comment "All Israelites have a share in the world to come."[2] Then follows a selection of the kind of actions that qualify this blanket statement. Most of these are acts of idolatry or denying the authority of the law of Moses. Then it is stated "But there are three kings and four commoners who have no share in the world to come. The three kings are Jeroboam, and Ahab and Manasseh [1 Kings 12:25–14:20; 16:29-34; 18:1–22:40, 2 Kings 21:1-18] . . . the four commoners are Baalam and Doeg and Ahithophel and Gehazi [Num. 22:1–24:25, 1 Sam. 21:7; 22:9-29, 2 Sam. 17:1-23, 2 Kings 5:19-27]." Of these seven, only one, Ahithophel, is among the Old Testament suicides, and even in his case, the rabbis excluded him from "the world to come" not because he was a suicide, but because he "betrayed his master," David. None of the other suicides is excluded from God's blessing in the afterlife.

In Saul's case, the text preserves no word of condemnation for the manner of his death. In fact, in David's heartfelt lament for Saul and Jonathan there is a deep sense of loss, of fond remembrance, and of hopes dashed, but no judgment for the suicide.

> Thy glory, O Israel, is slain upon thy high places!
>> How are the mighty fallen!
> Tell it not in Gath,
>> publish it not in the streets of Ashkelon;
> lest the daughters of the Philistines rejoice,
>> lest the daughters of the uncircumcised exult.

> Ye mountains of Gilboa,
>> let there be no dew or rain upon you,
>> nor upsurging of the deep!
> For there the shield of the mighty was defiled,
>> the shield of Saul, not anointed with oil.

> From the blood of the slain,
>> from the fat of the mighty,
> the bow of Jonathan turned not back,
>> and the sword of Saul returned not empty.

> Saul and Jonathan, beloved and lovely!
>> In life and in death they were not divided;
> they were swifter than eagles,
>> they were stronger than lions.

> Ye daughters of Israel, weep over Saul,
>> who clothed you daintily in scarlet,
>> who put ornaments of gold upon your apparel.

How are the mighty fallen
  in the midst of the battle!

Jonathan lies slain upon thy high places.
  I am distressed for you, my brother Jonathan;
very pleasant have you been to me;
  your love to me was wonderful,
  passing the love of women.

How are the mighty fallen,
  and the weapons of war perished!
(2 Sam. 1:19-27).

Even in the later Jewish writings, Saul is not condemned for suicide. The *Midrash Rabbah* is a rabbinic collection of oral traditions and interpretations that received its final editing between A.D. 1000 and 1050. In the comments on Leviticus 20:27,[3] there is a section which states that Saul:

> was slain for five sins: [1] as it says *He was unfaithful to the Lord in that he did not keep the command of the Lord* (1 Chron. 10:13) and [2] because he slew the inhabitants of Nob, the city of the priests [2 Sam. 22:11-23] and [3] because he spared Agag [1 Sam. 15:1-9] and [4] because he did not obey Samuel—for it says: *Seven days shalt thou tarry, untill I come unto thee* (1 Sam. 10:8), and he did not do so—and [5] because he inquired of the ghost and the familiar spirit [1 Sam. 28:3-20], *And inquired not of the Lord; therefore he slew him* (1 Chron. 10:14).

In an earlier part of this collection, the *Genesis Rabbah*, there are two other comments that bear on this issue. One is in the discussion of Genesis 9:5 where Saul (and Shadrach, Meshach and Abednego, the three Jews who put their lives in danger by refusing to worship an idol), are noted as exceptions to the general rule that the shedding of blood brings

God's judgment on the guilty person. The second is a comment on Genesis 21:28, where Abraham is told that the Philistines "will kill seven righteous men among your descendants, and these are they; Hophni, Phineas, Samson, Saul and his three sons." Samson, and Saul, of course, were suicides. Hophni and Phineas were the sons of the High Priest, Eli. According to the text in 1 Samuel 2:12-17, they were evil men who took bribes and misled the people. They were "sons of Belial [Satan]; they did not know the Lord." And yet they are counted as "righteous" just as Samson is listed among the heros of the faith in Hebrews 11.

In all these instances, there is not a single word of condemnation of these men for the *way* they died. Whether they were afflicted with delusions of grandeur and power like Zimri and Abimelech, remorseful traitors like Judas and Ahithophel, or divinely appointed leaders like Samson and Saul and his faithful armor-bearer, the biblical account records *no* negative judgment on them for their act of suicide. Rather, in every case, the deaths are treated simply as any other death would be. There are notes of horror and condemnation at some of their actions in life, and frequent references to their sins and shortcomings, but the manner of their deaths is not condemned as sinful.

It seems evident, then, that the biblical writers did not attach any particular guilt or sin to the act of suicide. They do not attach any moral judgment to the varying ways death comes. Death is death. The dead are separated from the living. The divide is crossed. Death may come in many different ways—by the action of an enemy army, or passing quietly to one's fathers at home in "a good old age," or in the shattered ruins of a destroyed palace, or by the deliberate, self-directed act of suicide. All deaths bring sorrow and despair, but the dead are buried, mourning is accomplished, and life goes on.

INTERMENT

Stinging
like a leather lash,
his words
ricochet off our stunned hearts
to that scar in the earth
and that desolate box—
the cold, cruel box
unbelievably cradling your ash.

CHAPTER EIGHT

WHAT THE CHURCH HAS SAID

Back in chapter 6 we noted that in much of the Christian church there is a strong belief that suicide is a very serious, or even an unforgivable, sin. However, as we examine the biblical accounts, we discover that there is no clear scriptural support for that view.

When we look beyond the Bible to the writings of the early church fathers, for the source behind this widespread idea, we find some rather startling things. Much of their writing is complicated and difficult to follow, even for those who are familiar with it, and it is certainly not easy for the lay person. Nevertheless, many of the beliefs and practices of the later church grow directly out of the teachings and writings of these early theologians. And it is for this reason I found it necessary to go back and reread the fathers. And again, as with the biblical material, I did not find what I expected.

What particularly surprised me was the discovery that the first Christian writer to condemn suicide explicitly was St. Augustine about the year A.D. 415.

In the early chapters of his book, *The City of God* (Book I, section 20),[1] Augustine argues that the sixth commandment, "Thou shalt not kill," prohibits suicide. He says:

> We have to understand that a man may not kill himself,
> since in the commandment "Thou shalt not kill" there is
> no limitation added, nor any exception made in favor of
> anyone, and least of all in favor of him on whom the
> command is laid! . . . the commandment is "Thou shalt
> not kill man," therefore neither another nor yourself, for
> he who kills himself still kills nothing else than a man.

But it is a curious fact that there is no evidence that any
writer before Augustine, either Jewish rabbi or Christian
teacher understood the sixth commandment to forbid suicide.

Certainly Augustine is technically accurate when he says
that "in the commandment 'Thou shalt not kill' there is no
limitation added, nor any exceptions made in favor of anyone." But he himself recognizes that in expressing his position in these terms he goes far beyond the biblical evidence.
No sooner has he made this blanket statement than he
hedges. "There are some exceptions made by the divine
authority to its own law, that men may not be put to death"
(section 21). The same divine law allows killing in war—in
fact specifically commands complete slaughter of peoples in
the holy war policy described in Deuteronomy. It further
instructs the Israelites to carry out capital punishment in certain clearly defined cases. Augustine identifies these exceptions as "being justified by a general law, or by a special
commission granted for a time to some individuals." Apart
from "these two classes of cases which are justified either by
a just law that applies generally, or by a special intimation
from God Himself, the fountain of all justice, whoever kills
a man, either himself or another, is implicated in the guilt of
murder" (section 21).

But immediately Augustine finds himself with a problem
case from the Old Testament—Samson, the Israelite judge
who is numbered with the great men of faith by the author
of the book of Hebrews. And Augustine proposes a rather

odd solution. This hero, "who drew down the house on him-self and his foes together, is justified only on this ground, that the Spirit who wrought wonders by him had given him secret instructions to do this" (section 21). Now this is an easy way out of the dilemma: the only reason Samson's death is not condemned is because God had given him "secret instructions" to kill himself. We will return to the Samson episode shortly, as Augustine uses this idea again in dis-cussing some of the saints of the church, but before we do, there is another area to consider.

Apart from the fact that the commandment in Exodus 20:13 says simply "Thou shalt not kill," not "Thou shalt not kill man," the concern is a valid one and Augustine's argu-ment needs to be examined in the context in which he him-self set it. Much of the material in this part of *The City of God* (sections 16-29) deals with female prisoners, either vir-gin or married, who find themselves actual or potential vic-tims of rape or other sexual abuse in times of persecution at the hands of pagan soldiers or slave owners. For many of these women, the choice was either to live with the shame of the degradation or to take their own lives as a way of escap-ing the dishonor.

At this point, Augustine finds himself with another major problem. He first discusses the well-known case of the prominent Roman matron, Lucretia, who had committed suicide after being raped by the son of King Tarquin. In Roman society Lucretia was praised as a virtuous woman who had put herself to death because she could not endure the shame of what had been done to her.

Augustine's examination of the case involves two points: either (1) Lucretia was innocent of any wrongdoing in the seduction she suffered, in which case she murdered an inno-cent woman—herself—by her suicide, or (2) she may have given secret consent to the sexual union, even though it was rape, in which case she was an adulteress. This sets up a dilemma: Lucretia was either a murderer (if innocent), or an adulteress (if guilty). "If she was adulterous, why praise her? If chaste, why slay her?"[2]

At first glance this story about Lucretia seems like an unnecessary diversion. But for Augustine, the parallel between this episode and numerous instances of similar events in the history of the church presents a serious dilemma. There are a number of accounts of Christian women who jumped to their deaths from high places or had drowned themselves in rivers in order to avoid sexual violation. These women are venerated in the Catholic church as saints and martyrs in spite of their self-inflicted deaths. At this point Augustine finds himself torn between his understanding of the command against murder and the church's approval of these acts of martyrdom. But beyond that, Augustine also faced a difficult personal situation.

In 384, nearly forty years before he wrote *The City of God,* Augustine had moved to Milan to become instructor of philosophy and rhetoric. At that time he was still hostile to Christianity, but at Milan he came under the influence of the bishop, Ambrose, who was world-famous for his preaching skills. Augustine, as a teacher of public speaking, was curious to discover why Ambrose was so effective as a communicator. After listening to him for some months, Augustine came to realize that the reason for Ambrose's power as an orator was that he really believed what he was proclaiming. And gradually Augustine became convinced of the truth of what Ambrose was saying, not just impressed by the way he was saying it. That conviction of the truth of the message finally led Augustine to convert to Christianity. He was baptized by Ambrose at Easter in the year 387.

In A.D. 377, ten years before Augustine's conversion, Ambrose had written a major treatise, *Concerning Virgins,*[3] in which he discussed and defended the widespread practice of celibacy. One chapter of that treatise retells the story of St. Pelagia, her sisters, and their mother, who, in order to avoid persecution, drowned themselves in a river. These women are counted as saints by the church, and in this light, Ambrose is confident that martyrdom, even though the way it is achieved is self-inflicted, is wholly in keeping with holiness. It is not to be condemned.

Augustine is not at ease with this conclusion. He recognizes that self-inflicted death, even though in the name of obedience to the faith, is suicide. He cannot condone such self-murder. But he is unwilling to reject the tradition of his church and the writing of so eminent a leader as Ambrose by repudiating the actions of these women. He writes:

> Of such persons I do not presume to speak rashly. I cannot tell whether there may not have been vouchsafed to the church some divine authority, proved by trustworthy evidences, for so honouring their memory: it may be that it is so. It may be they were not deceived by human judgement, but prompted by divine wisdom, to their act of self-destruction. We know that this was the case with Samson. And when God enjoins any act, and intimates by plain evidence that He has enjoined it, who will call obedience criminal? Who will accuse so religious a submission?

Just as Augustine had argued that Samson was "secretly instructed" by God to take his own life, he now suggests that these women were also "prompted by divine wisdom" to commit suicide.

Yet Augustine, in spite of his unwillingness to contradict his mentor, Ambrose, and with every effort to justify the honoring of these martyrs and Old Testament heroes, concluded this section of the *The City of God* with these words:

> This we affirm, this we maintain, this we every way pronounce to be right, that no man ought to inflict upon himself voluntary death, for this is to escape the ills of time by plunging into those of eternity; that no man ought to do so on account of another man's sins;

for this were to escape a guilt which could not pollute
him, by incurring great guilt of his own; that no man
ought to do so on account of his own past sins, for he
has all the more need of this life that these sins may be
healed by repentance; that no man should put an end to
this life to obtain that better life we look for after
death, for those who die by their own hand have no
better life after death.

Augustine's position is clear and unmistakable, and has
been accepted to a very large degree by most Christian writers since. But there are two problems here. (1) What evidence
is there of these secret instructions to Samson or to these
martyrs? (2) What evidence is there that any (every?) other
suicide did not also have these secret instructions? Of course
"secret" by definition means unknown to those not in on the
secret. But the Bible says nothing about supernatural instructions to its suicides—it just records the events. Augustine's
reason proves nothing, and at the same time proves too
much. Any suicide, whether Samson's, the early martyrs, or
the one that happened yesterday can be excused on the
grounds that "God gave secret instructions" to the victim to
take his own life.

It is of interest that in the article on suicide in *The New
Catholic Encyclopedia*, the author comments:

> If suicide is intrinsically evil, God could not command
> it, and it is not true, as some have alleged, that direct
> suicide is permissible if it is committed in response to a
> special inspiration of God, the Lord of life and death.
> This is a solution proposed by some to explain the sui-
> cides of certain holy virgins who killed themselves in
> defense of their virtue. However virtue can be ade-
> quately defended by other means than suicide, and a
> woman who is forcibly violated does not, on that
> account, lose her virtue. Hence these acts can only be
> justified by attributing them to inculpable ignorance.[4]

The author of the article was faced with the same problem as Augustine, but was not willing to accept Augustine's solution. Nor is he willing to identify the "some" with whom he disagrees as Ambrose, Augustine, and Aquinas, three of the most influential theologians in the church. Unfortunately, he offers no alternatives, and the question remains. If suicide is "intrinsically evil" and the acts of the martyrs are the result of ignorance, by what criteria are these women admitted to sainthood?

HER TIME

Some said it was her time:
as if the rhyme
of life
dismissed a beat
just short enough to take her.

Some judged it was her time:
as if the bloom
of life
had failed to fruit,
and nothing could remake her.

You knew it was her time:
and that December's crime
of cutting life
precluded spring,

and we shall never wake her.

CHAPTER NINE

ABOUT THE MARTYRS

In the pagan society in which Augustine lived and worked, there was a long-standing tradition of great heroes, both men and women, who were willing to die for their country or their convictions. It is not surprising, then, that the early Christians, whose absolute confidence in the resurrection from the dead totally controlled their actions, were equally willing to face death for their beliefs.

Since the earliest days of the Christian church, there have been times of serious persecution, and there are many instances of believers being executed for their faith. The stories of the martyrs have long been a matter of great interest to many people both inside and outside the church. Stories and stage plays, movies and TV dramas have made even our own generation familiar with gladiators, the arenas, and the wild animals. The saying "Like a Christian to the lions" still needs little explanation.

Beginning with the killing of Stephen (Acts 7:54-60) sometime before A.D. 40, the bloody story unfolds. According to one line of tradition, all the apostles except John died violent deaths as martyrs. John himself, according to the story, was miraculously delivered safe and unharmed from a cauldron of boiling oil, but all the others, including Paul, died violently at the hands of their enemies. Then under a series of Roman emperors—from Nero, Domitian, and Trajan in the first and second centuries to Diocletian and Galerius at the beginning of the fourth century—thousands if not tens of thousands of Christians, both men and women from all ranks of life, faced death by martyrdom in the arenas with the wild beasts and the gladiators, or at the hands of the public executioners by sword, crucifixion, or other painful torture.

In the Christian community, however, it was not until the beginning of the second century that the desire for death and the deliberate courting of it by martyrdom appears in the literature. The word translated *witness* in the New Testament is the Greek word *martyr*. It simply means "bear witness" or, more colloquially, "tell what you know about something." But by the middle of the second century there was a very large group in the church who believed that the only true way to be a *witness* for the Christian faith was to be a *martyr*—that is, to *witness* by *death*.

One of the earliest of these accounts outside the New Testament is that of Ignatius, bishop of Antioch, who was put to death by the Roman authorities in the year A.D. 107. We know next to nothing about his early years or his ministry, except that he ministered in Antioch during the reign of the Emperor Domitian who was responsible for the persecution described so graphically by John in the book of Revelation. Under Domitian's successor Trajan, severe persecution of the Christians continued in parts of the Empire, and it was during this time that Ignatius was arrested, tried, and sentenced to death. As he was being taken to Rome for execution, he wrote a series of letters to various churches and individuals in cities along his route. Several times in these letters he expresses the desire to "attain unto God" and to arrive at the point where he is "found to be a disciple." The letters are full of concern lest these friends intervene in his case and somehow get him freed. But he discourages this idea, for Ignatius believes true discipleship is possible only if he meets death as a martyr.

Ignatius's letters[1] abound with death language: "hoping

through your prayers to succeed in fighting with the wild beasts in Rome";[2] "I desire to suffer";[3] "Near to the sword, near to God; in company with wild beasts, in company with God."[4] But it is especially in his letter to the Romans that his desire for death is clearly set out: "Grant me nothing more than that I be poured out as a libation to God while there is still an altar ready"; "Let me be given to the wild beasts, for through them I can attain unto God. I am God's wheat and am ground by the teeth of wild beasts. . . . Supplicate the Lord for me that through these instruments I may be found a sacrifice to God"; "May I have joy of the beasts that have been prepared for me"; "I write to you in the midst of life, yet lusting after death."[5] Then he makes his position absolutely clear: "I bid all men know that of my own free will I die for God."[6] Ignatius's letters encouraged a whole host of other Christians to follow his example.

As the Roman empire, faced with moral and social problems internally and increasingly threatened by external enemies, struggled to maintain some semblance of control over its people and territory, the political leadership turned to more and more arbitrary measures. Exile, slavery, torture, and execution were some of the means by which they attempted to enforce compliance. And among the many groups of people who were seen as a threat to the public safety, the Christians were the most visible. It was not that the Christians were an armed threat or a group of evil doers. Nor was it in their refusal to live by most of the laws of the realm. The central problem was that the Christians refused to acknowledge that the ruling emperor deserved to be worshiped as a god. They would not say, "Caesar is Lord."

Pliny, a local governor in Bithynia during Trajan's reign, describes in a report to the Emperor how he had handled the trial of those accused of being Christians:

> I interrogated them whether they were Christians; if they confessed it I repeated the question twice again,

adding the threat of capital punishment; if they still persevered, I ordered them to be executed. For whatever the
nature of their creed might be, I could at least feel no
doubt that contumacy and inflexible obstinacy deserved
chastisement. . . . those who denied they were, or had
ever been Christians, who repeated after me an invocation to the gods, and offered adoration, with wine and
frankincense, to your image, which I had ordered to be
brought for the purpose, together with those of the gods,
and who finally cursed Christ—none of which acts, it is
said, those who are really Christians can be forced into
performing—these I thought it proper to discharge.
Others . . . at first confessed themselves Christians, and
then denied it; true, they had been of that persuasion but
had quitted it. . . . They all worshipped your statue and
the images of the gods, and cursed Christ.[7]

While this is a local report dealing particularly with the situation in Bithynia, similar situations were occurring in many
other parts of the empire. Many Christians from many different places were treated in very similar fashion.

It was then just a short step from submitting to such
treatment to actively seeking confrontation with the authorities. And more and more the ideas that Ignatius had
expressed were accepted. Deliberately choosing death was
seen as the purest and best expression of the Christian faith.
It is evident, of course, that in most of these cases, it was still
execution for offenses against the state, not self-inflicted suicide as a result of personal failure that is the issue. But the
record is absolutely clear that in very many instances the
"victim" deliberately courted death.

It is against that backdrop that Augustine's work is set.
His concern in *The City of God* is first of all to make it clear
to his readers that deliberately seeking death is not the best,
nor even an appropriate way to demonstrate one's faith. So
he spells out his position that suicide—"death by one's own
free choice"—is a grave sin.

Given the historical situation he was in, Augustine's desire to resolve the issue is understandable. However, his solution is marred by two considerations: (1) a rather fuzzy and less-than-adequate logical argument,[8] and (2) his appeal to the murder commandment which is without precedent anywhere in the earlier literature. Nevertheless, Augustine's teaching became the official stance of the church from about A.D. 450 right down to the present day.

MY TIME

I've had my time
—the coldest months.
Convinced no green
survived the meanness
I thought mourning had no end.
Grief, like ice, embraced me,
and numbness,
like December.

I had forgotten the thawing
and the robin,
the buds, and the blossoming
of the dead.

CHAPTER 10

WHAT THE THEOLOGIANS SAY

While it was Augustine who first linked the command "Thou shalt not kill" with the prohibition against suicide, it was Thomas Aquinas, a Dominican monk and "Doctor of the Church" who lived from A.D. 1225 to 1274, who developed the theological statement.

Aquinas wrote a series of books called the *Summa Theologica* in which he combined the traditional teachings preserved in the church fathers with the ideas of the Greek philosopher Aristotle (384-322 B.C.) whose writings had just been newly rediscovered. The *Summa* is still the primary statement of Roman Catholic teaching.

In his treatment of suicide,[1] Aquinas begins by first quoting Augustine as the primary authority and then proceeds to add three additional arguments. Suicide is always a mortal sin because: (1) it is a denial of the self-love for life that every being naturally has; (2) suicide is the rejection of one's obligations to the community; and (3) since life is God-given, only God can take it back.

The first and third of these reasons are taken directly from the writings of the Jewish historian Josephus,[2] although Aquinas does not acknowledge this source; the second reason is directly from Aristotle. These three reasons have been the chief focus of attention by those who have written about suicide since Aquinas. The official position of the Catholic Church is in line with Aquinas's point of view, but not all authors have come to similar conclusions or agreement. For this reason, there are several issues that need to be examined.

Aquinas's first reason is a double one: (a) Suicide is a sin because it is contrary to the "natural law" that every being naturally tries to preserve its life as long as possible; and (b) self-destruction is contrary to the self-love which Jesus commands "Love your neighbor as *yourself*" (Matt. 19:19). These two elements are closely linked, and at first glance, seem to be compelling. But they assume what is very frequently not true.

There are many people for whom the idea of death is *not* something to be avoided. Life itself—for a whole variety of reasons—can be seen as itself an evil which must be escaped. There may be those like the martyrs for whom the comments of Ignatius, "I bid all men know that of my own free will I die for God," give exactly that viewpoint. Here is a devout Christian leader—a bishop in one of the most important churches of his day—whose "own free will" is set toward death. He, and countless others like him, saw this life and the reality of this physical existence as hindrances to full spiritual growth.

Then, too, the whole idea of "self-love" is one which gives many people, major difficulty. In many branches of the Christian church, the overriding emphasis on our sinfulness and our complete inability to earn favor with God, coupled with the constant urging to put the good of others ahead of oneself (the old cliché we all learned in youth group: "The way to JOY is Jesus first, Others second, Yourself last") reinforces the idea that love of self is a very serious sin. Of course selfishness and self-centeredness are indeed sins, because the center of life for the Christian is Christ himself. But within that Christ-centered life there is the reality that it is one's

Production of *Fierce Goodbye* documentary

Photos by Wayne Gehman, Burton Buller, and Jim Bowman

The documentary, *Fierce Goodbye: Living in the Shadow of Suicide*, was produced by Mennonite Media with Faith & Values Media to air on the Hallmark Channel.

Dr. G. Lloyd Carr, professor emeritus of biblical studies at Gordon College and his wife, **Gwendolyn,** a poet, stroll the wintry shore near Magnolia, Mass., a walk Gwendolyn frequently enjoyed with her daughter-in-law before the young woman ended her life. The title for the book comes from a poem by Gwendolyn, which the Carrs graciously allowed to be adopted for the documentary.

Jill Ann Marks, a licensed holistic psychologist from Minneapolis, Minn., discusses production with Burton Buller, director/producer. Jim Bowman, videographer, lines up camera angles in the Minneapolis cemetery where Jill's daughter, Jamie is buried.

Ila and Merle Brubaker, Camp Hill, Pa., lost their twin son, Darrel, after a deep depression stemming in part from his concern for victims of sexual abuse by a professional counselor.

Barbara and Jonas Borntrager, Harrisonburg, Va., meditate at the gravesite of their son, Jon, who was 21 when he died from a drug overdose after several suicide attempts. Jon suffered from Turret's Syndrome throughout his adolescent and teenage years.

Stephen Akinduro, Columbus, Ga., was nine years old when his mother took her life. The Akinduros lived at that time in Nigeria after meeting in the U.S. and navigating the difficulties of a cross-cultural marriage.

Fred Davis, Asheville, N.C., was a state trooper when his 15-year-old daughter impulsively took her life in the throes of a painful romance. Out of his anguish Fred and his wife, Joyce, founded P.A.T.S., a hotline for teenagers considering suicide.

Dr. Fred and Gail Fox, Harrisonburg, Va., pause in their backyard near a simple marker for their son who died by suicide without any real prior signs or warning. The Foxes founded a chapter of Compassionate Friends for persons losing a child and have addressed suicide issues for the American Society of Suicidology.

Resource persons for the documentary:

Dr. Kay Redfield Jamison, professor of psychiatry at Johns Hopkins University, Baltimore, Md., author of *Night Falls Fast* and numerous other books, and diagnosed with bipolar disorder.

Dr. James T. Clemons, professor emeritus of New Testament from Wesley Theological Seminary in Washington, D.C., and founder of the Organization for Attempters and Survivors of Suicide in Inter-Faith Services (OASSIS).

Dr. Sherry Davis Molock, associate professor of psychology, George Washington University, Washington, D.C.

Dr. Donna Holland Barnes, a suicide sociologist for the department of psychiatry at Howard University, Washington, D.C., and founder of National Organization for People of Color Against Suicide (NOPCAS).

Rabbi Daniel A. Roberts, rabbi emeritus of Temple Emanu El, Cleveland, Ohio, and producer of a video on teenage suicide, "Inside I Ache."

Rabbi Marcia Zimmerman, senior rabbi at Temple Israel, Minneapolis, Minn.

Rev. Stanley S. Harakas, a priest of the Greek Orthodox Archdiocese of America, is Archbishop Iakovos Professor of Orthodox Theology, Emeritus, Holy Cross Greek Orthodox School of Theology, Brookline, Mass.

The documentary team also thanks many persons appearing in the documentary with supplemental interviews and commentary. In addition, a debt of gratitude to the many other individuals interviewed for the documentary formally and informally which, while the interview segments were not used in the actual documentary for reasons of length, served as important background research and source material for the research process and the in-depth website resource found at **www.fiercegoodbye.com.**

own life that Christ has brought to fulfillment. Jesus himself, was the one who said "You shall love your neighbor as yourself" (Matt. 19:19; Lev. 19:18). In spite of these words of Jesus, though, many of his followers have very little self-love and as a result, a very low self-image.

In retrospect, it is obvious to us that this was Kate's situation. Although she was a woman of considerable talent and had a genuine gift for organization, a deep sense of personal inadequacy was constantly with her. Any minor failure was seen as total disaster and left her with the feeling that her whole world was about to collapse. These all-too-common problems were compounded for Kate by her inability finally to break the drug and alcohol addiction she shared with countless other young people of the late 1960s. Like so many of her peers from that lost generation, she was seduced by the lying promises of the gurus of free love and drug-induced escapism. And even when she encountered the gospel and was confronted with the claims of Christ in her life, the struggle continued.

Her commitment was genuine, and, in the first few years of her conversion, her life showed many signs of growth and progress in the faith, yet the old habits died hard. Nor was the task made any easier for her by the indoctrination of some of her friends, who taught her to think that if she only had "enough faith" all her problems would disappear. She tried to follow their lead, but when the problems would not disappear and the old temptations proved so strong, she found herself thinking that in fact she did not have enough faith, nor could she ever get "enough."

Such are the wiles of the Adversary of the soul. We are human, and what we are is still colored and influenced by what we have been. For most of us, the Christian life is a series of steps forward and slips back. The ideal is complete and perfect deliverance in one glorious Damascus Road experience. The reality is still scales on the eyes, the thorn in the flesh, and Christ's sufficient grace. (Acts 9:1-18; 2 Cor.

12:7-9). But for Kate, like so many others, the scales and the thorns so hid the grace that reality ended in lost confidence and deep despair. Death seemed less threatening than the task of trying to untangle all the knotted threads of her life and psyche.

Those who have studied suicide from a psychological or social perspective generally place depression and strong feelings of personal inadequacy high on the list of personality problems of those who commit suicide. It is not surprising, then, that Christians sometimes resort to destroying themselves when their sense of love for themselves and for life is destroyed. Monica Dickens once wrote, "Suicide is the chosen escape from pain when there seems to be no other choice nor hope of one." To those for whom life is so disoriented and the difficulties of day-to-day existence are so overwhelming, death often seems to offer the only possible solution. Admittedly, the despair that drives a person to suicide may be wildly misguided, but its reality is beyond question.

The pain may be physical, emotional, or psychological, but when that level of hurt combines with a deep sense of personal worthlessness, even Christians can resort to suicide. Here, the "mortal sin" is not, as Aquinas states, the act of suicide. The sin that makes mortal life unbearable, is earlier —the more pervasive lack of an appropriate Christian self-love.

John Donne, the famous English poet and writer of the early 1600s, and an ordained priest in the Church of England, has among his many books one on suicide,[3] in which he examines the arguments of Augustine and Aquinas in light of the history of suicide and martyrdom in the early church, and then goes on to discuss, at considerable length, the work of other writers on the topic up to his own time. In discussing Aquinas's concept of the "natural law," Donne examines the words of Paul in Romans 2:14-15 where the Apostle describes the Gentiles as "doing by nature" what "the law [of Moses] requires." Donne concludes that if

Paul's words are true, "every act which concurs not exactly with our religion shall be sin against nature." He describes the taking of medicine to combat sickness, or surgery to heal wounds as "against nature" (i.e. to prevent death), and summarizes his argument with the comment that "whether it be against reason or no . . . the self-homicide is no more against the law of nature than any other sin." Donne has demonstrated with Aquinas the same problem we noted above with Augustine and the "secret command" idea. The solution proposed by Aquinas destroys itself by undercutting the ground of its own argument.

Aquinas's second reason, that suicide "injures the community," has, at face value, a very strong element of truth. The death of any member of a community brings a deep sense of grief and loss. This is especially true of the death of a young person whose promised achievement is never realized. And all of this is compounded in the case of an accidental death or of suicide. However, Aquinas's argument here is not based on any scriptural material but on the words of "The Philosopher." Most scholars identify his reference here with the *Nicomachean Ethics*[4] where Aristotle writes:

> He who kills himself in a fit of passion, voluntarily, does an injury (against the right principle [of "retaliation"]) which the law does not allow. Therefore the suicide commits injustice; but against whom? It seems to be against the *state* [my italics] rather than against himself; for he suffers voluntarily and nobody suffers injustice voluntarily. This is why the state exacts a penalty; a suicide is punished by certain marks of dishonor, as being an offence against the state.[5]

In essence, Aristotle condemns suicide because, the suicide, by his self-destructive act, deprives the state of a taxpayer and a soldier.

There are two important problem areas to be noted here.

Aquinas, of course, was writing in the thirteenth century A.D. in a society where there was no essential difference between the state—the Holy Roman Empire—and the Catholic Church. This political/ecclesiastical reality had been more or less in force in Europe for nearly 900 years. And for nearly 900 years the line separating the political and religious spheres implied in our Lord's injunction, "Give to Caesar what is Caesar's and to God what is God's" had been blurred to the point of indistinguishability. So ingrained was this idea that Aquinas and his followers failed to realize the totally pagan ideology which lay behind Aristotle's argument.

The pagan philosopher is reflecting the pagan philosophy that the political state is the ultimate authority and has ultimate control over the life and destiny of its people. It was against this outrageous claim that the early Christians reacted. Reflecting their strong Hebrew roots, they refused to acknowledge the claims of the political powers over their own consciences. Because these early Christians knew and proclaimed "The Lord Jesus" they constantly found themselves in conflict with the Roman authorities who demanded that they acknowledge "The Lord Caesar." Where pagan Rome had used her political power to try to force all the people, Christians included, into submission to her claims to control every area of life, so in the middle ages, "Christian" Rome used her religious power to try to force all people, Christians, Jews, and pagans alike, to submit to her claims to control every area of life. Aquinas failed to see that the very basis of his argument was in direct conflict with the biblical standards and point of view.

The central problem with Aquinas's approach here, however, is his apparent acceptance of Aristotle's argument "nobody suffers injustice voluntarily." If Aristotle and Aquinas are correct on this point, then the whole Christian message is false. For the heart of the gospel of Christ is that Jesus willingly and consciously suffered injustice at the hands of the political and religious leaders. He was betrayed by a disciple, arrested, tried, mocked, beaten, and finally executed as a common criminal. And still he was able to say, "I lay down my life, that I may take it again. No one takes it from me, but I lay it down of my own accord. I have power to lay it down, and I have power to take it again" (John 10:17-18). He went to the cross, deliberately laying down his life. Now it is no good arguing, "But that's different." If the *principle* Aristotle is proposing is *true,* then it must apply in Jesus' case. If it is not true for Jesus, there is no justifiable ground for using this idea as an argument against either martyrdom or suicide. And in fact, the whole history of the church is studded with examples of faithful men and women who "suffered injustice voluntarily."

It is only in Aquinas's third point that we get back to a semblance of biblical thinking. Life is God's gift (Gen. 2:7) and he alone is able to make alive. We will look at this issue more closely in the next chapter, but before we do so, it is important that we examine Aquinas's argument in some detail. When we do so, it becomes evident that he makes some unfortunate assumptions in his handling of the biblical text.

Aquinas develops his argument in terms of a passage in the Old Testament in Deuteronomy 32:39, "I kill and I make alive." He takes this as the basis for arguing that to kill oneself is a sin against God, just as to kill another man's slave is a sin—not against the slave—but against the master! The logic of this is muddled, but even more unfortunate is the way in which Aquinas ignores the context in which these words occur.

Deuteronomy 32 is a "song" of Moses describing Israel's sin against God. God's judgment is to come on the nation because they have forgotten their allegiance to "the God who gave them birth" [as a nation] (v. 18) and turned away to worship "strange gods" (v. 16).

Because of this sin, God promises to bring judgment on his people (Israel) at the hand of a people "who are no people . . . a foolish nation" (v. 21), who think that it is by their own power they will have destroyed Israel. "Our hand is triumphant, the Lord [of Israel] has not wrought all this" (v. 27). But God calls these conquerors a nation with "no understanding in them" (v. 28). They have failed to recognize that they are victorious over Israel *only because* God has chosen them to judge *his own people*. These nations will do the job God has assigned them, and they will, in turn, be brought under the same judgment for *their* failure to recognize the true God.

It is in this context that verse 39 is set: "See now that I, even I, am he, and that there is no god beside me; I kill and I make alive; I wound and I heal; and there is none that can deliver out of my hand." This is good Hebrew poetry, set up in what is called a chiastic form. The word "chiastic" is a technical term that means that the poet is expressing two parts of one idea in two different ways, and the second time he reverses the order of the parts. This form is described as "a . b : b . a" order. The two middle parts "I kill and I make alive," and "I wound and I heal," are parallel statements with the same meaning. Similarly, the two "a" parts also say the same thing—God—the only real, living God, cannot be evaded.

When we look at the verse as a whole, the word order "I kill and I make alive; I wound and I heal" is important in the context. Note it is not "I make alive and I kill"—which is what would be necessary for Aquinas's understanding that this text describes the individual. What the poet is saying is that Israel as a *nation* has been given birth by God (vv. 6, 18) and raised to a place of honor and blessing. Yet Israel sinned—sinned unto death—and God was forced to bring judgment on the *nation*. "I kill." Yet once the judgment had fallen on the disobedient people, the faithful remnant will be restored—"I make alive"—and the dry bones of the lost people will live again (cf. Ezek. 37:5-6). Moses's appeal here is to God as the creator of all nations and peoples, and the clear point is made that God is in control of all the affairs of all people. The order is destruction then restoration, not life then death. To take this part of the verse as a reason or proof text against suicide is to ignore the clear meaning of the passage in its larger context.

Nevertheless, Aquinas, like Augustine, shaped the thinking of many later theologians. His treatment is still widely accepted as the true, authoritative interpretation held by the church.

A TIME TO CRY

This is the time
when lips hide words
behind the desolation;
when only tears
tell truth.

This is the time
that one must say
what must be said
about one's self
about the dead.

But if denial caps
this painful welling,
then truth is turned
and time is left
untasted.

CHAPTER ELEVEN

LIFE AND DEATH

D ietrich Bonhoeffer, the great German theologian who was executed in a Nazi concentration camp in April, 1945, describes suicide as "the self-accomplished expiation for a life that has failed . . . the attempt to give a final human meaning to a life which has become humanly meaningless."[1] While many of Bonhoeffer's fellow prisoners did resort to suicide in the agony and degradation of the death camps, he himself counseled against that way of escape from the misery. But when life is unbearable, and there seems to be no hope of deliverance, death, even self-inflicted, can be seen as liberation.

This is the final element in Aquinas's argument against suicide that needs to be examined. He writes, "It is not lawful for man to take his own life that he may pass to a happier life, nor that he may escape any unhappiness whatsoever of the present life, because the ultimate and most fearsome evil of this life is death as the Philosopher states." But once again we need to observe that this perspective is a pagan, Greek idea, not a biblical, Hebrew, nor Christian one.

Aquinas is referring to Aristotle's discussion of the virtue of courage where he says, "there is no one more brave in enduring danger than the courageous man. Now the most terrible thing of all is death; for it is the end, and when a man is dead, nothing, we think, either good or evil can befall him any more."[2] Aristotle then moves to a discussion of "noble death," and concludes that "death in battle" is the noblest, "for it is encountered in the midst of the greatest and most noble of dangers."

One may or may not agree with Aristotle's position that death in battle is the most noble form of death, but no Christian can accept the idea that "the most terrible thing of all is death." Aquinas would have been closer to the Christian understanding had he followed Augustine's lead.

> Of this, at least I am certain, that no one has ever died that was not destined to die some time. . . . Death is not to be judged an evil which is the end of a good life; for death becomes evil only by the retribution which follows it. They, then, who are destined to die, need not be careful to inquire what death they are to die, but into what place death will usher them.

All the evidence from the history of the New Testament church makes it absolutely clear that while life is a God-given gift to be enjoyed and used in God's service, there is no trace of Aristotle's idea that life was to be preserved at all costs.

> We shall be quite clear that nothing was further from the minds of the early Christians than to condemn a self-inflicted death in the name of any loyalty to our own personal existence. The contempt for life among the early Christians was so extreme that to modern eyes it might sometimes seem even monstrous.[3]

It was our Lord himself who declared "Do not fear those who kill the body but cannot kill the soul; rather fear him who can destroy both soul and body in hell" (Matt. 10:28). No, in this case Aristotle and Aquinas are simply wrong.

George MacDonald, in a letter to his stepmother following the death of his sister Bella at the age of fourteen, wrote: "Schiller says 'Death cannot be an evil because it is universal.'

God would not let it be the Law of His Universe if it were what it looks to us."[4] At first glance, Schiller (and MacDonald) appear to be in direct contradiction to the biblical teaching. But are they really?

Certainly, according to the account in Genesis 2:15-17 and 3:1-24, death was the penalty imposed on Adam and Eve for disobeying God's command not to eat of the fruit of the tree of knowledge of good and evil. And all of us, like them, have been similarly disobedient (Rom. 5:12-14), and death has come on us all. But actually, in a real sense, MacDonald was right. For even though death is the penalty of sin, and is in fact "the last enemy" (1 Cor. 15:26), it is also the one guarantee that we will not live for eternity in a sin-cursed world. Adam and Eve were driven from the garden specifically to keep them from gaining access to the fruit of the tree of life (Gen. 3:22). Had the disobedient pair eaten of that fruit also, the hell of a sin-cursed eternity would be the only option for us all. God, in his mercy provided death, so that redemption becomes possible. We all must die, but there is the promise of resurrection, the hope of the gospel. The last enemy *will* be overcome.

This is a liberating perspective. The one reality we all face, apart from the Lord's return, is our own physical death. One birth, one death is the ultimate statistical reality. Wise is the believer who recognizes that fact, but who likewise refuses to let that knowledge destroy the joy of day-to-day living. C. S. Lewis reminds us that:

> If we are all going to be destroyed by an atomic bomb, let that bomb when it comes find us doing sensible and human things—praying, working, teaching, reading, listening to music, bathing the children, playing tennis, chatting to our friends over a pint and a game of darts—not huddled together like frightened sheep and thinking about bombs. They may break our bodies (a microbe can do that) but they need not dominate our minds.[5]

Our Lord himself told us "Do not worry about tomorrow: tomorrow will take care of itself. Each day has enough trouble of its own" (Matt. 6:34, *Jerusalem Bible*). Christianity has not been led to condemn suicide from any attachment to earthly life or from any particularly exalted view of its value.[6]

The Old Testament story of Job reminds us that there is another side to this problem. It was Job, when confronted with the reality of the loss of his children, his servants, and all his possessions, confessed his submission to God. "The Lord gave, and the Lord has taken away; blessed be the name of the Lord" (Job 1:20). Too often these words of Job's become the platitude we use to comfort those who mourn. Death after a lengthy illness, death in battle, death by accident or gratuitous violence we can comprehend. And even of death by murder we can say "The Lord has taken." But can we—*dare* we—say of the suicide "The *Lord* has taken . . . "?

For those who face the aftermath of suicide the question is a painfully practical one, but the question cannot be limited only to those suffering such loss. There is a profound theological issue that needs examination. At the bottom it is a question of the interrelated doctrines of divine sovereignty and human freewill. On the one hand, there are those theologians who place such emphasis on divine sovereignty (or "fate"), that the individual, predestined to specific actions and conditions from the foundation of the world, is in reality nothing more than a puppet in the hands of some divine puppeteer or a pawn in the hands of blind chance. At the other extreme there are those, both Christian and secular, who will allow nothing more than natural phenomena and personal choice as the controlling factors.

The truth lies somewhere between. Nowhere in the Bible is there any suggestion that an individual is *not* responsible for his or her actions. But it is equally true that the Bible nowhere suggests that God is not in total control of both the affairs of each individual and the affairs of the whole universe. And that is the problem. Somehow we must reconcile these two truths. We must say that the suicide is responsible for the act that snuffs out life, but we must *not* say also, that, by that act, God's sovereign plan for the individual was frustrated and destroyed. To live in the tension of these two beliefs is difficult, but it must be done if we are to be faithful to the whole teaching of Scripture. Even in the case of suicide we *must* say "The Lord has taken. . . ."

But that confession raises two other problems. The first has to do with the ultimate result of the suicide on the lives of the survivors. There is, of course, the initial shock of sudden death and the trauma that brings. There is the grief and sense of helpless loss. There may be the overwhelming sense of abandonment coupled with expressed or hidden anger. "How could he do this to me!" "How could she abandon our children!" And so on and on. But the reality is that they have. And when we come to face the reality, we often discover that the impact is not all negative.

In the case of the suicide of one suffering from a terminal illness, the suicidal act may in fact spare the family months or years of debilitating sorrow and hardship that still end in the death of the sufferer. There have been documented cases of some sort of deep-seated mental illness such as schizophrenia where the sufferer, in more lucid moments, believes suicide to be the only sure way to avoid doing unintended violence against innocent people. Then too, there are those cases where the death of the suicide victim is the resolution to a long-standing problem within the family. The constant upheaval and turmoil of conflict or the destructive influence of depression both on the victim and those around him are suddenly removed by the suicide. Of course, all of these decisions may be correct, or they may be wildly misguided. There may have been other resolutions to the problems that would have been equally effective but without the loss of the life of the suicide. But the results, often even in the short term, are for the good of the survivors even though the suicide is real, and the shock is devastating.

The second problem that arises from the confession "The Lord has taken" relates to Jesus' words in Matthew 10:28 quoted above. "Do not fear those who kill the body but cannot kill the soul; rather fear him who can destroy both soul and body in hell." A common understanding of this passage is that Jesus is warning us to fear Satan. But in fact, as an examination of the context shows, Jesus is warning us here to fear God. It is God who ultimately divides the sheep from the goats, the believers from the unbelievers, the redeemed from the condemned. And the person who is truly living in awe of God will not be awed by any thing or any one lesser.

Further, there is Jesus' observation that killing the body does not mean killing the soul—the real person. One may destroy the body, the physical self, but that is all one does—destroy the *body*. The person, the self, is still living in God's presence. And the promise of the resurrection is the certainty of the reuniting of the soul with the glorified, resurrected body.

Bonhoeffer argues that suicide is not the sin of murder, but the sin of lack of faith. This is not a moral failure, because both good and bad actions can reflect lack of faith. It is that lack, he says, which "takes no account of the living God. That is the sin." Survivors of the death camps testify that it was those who maintained their faith, who refused to succumb to despair, who were more likely to survive. Those who lost faith, either in themselves or in God, were the most likely casualties. They felt that God had abandoned them in their time of trial and need, and so resorted to death. But this way out is not a release. "Lack of faith is disastrous in that it conceals from a man the fact that even suicide cannot release him from the hand of God who has prepared his destiny for him. Lack of faith does not perceive, beyond the gift of bodily life, the Creator and Lord who alone has the right to dispose of his creation."[7]

Nevertheless, no one who has had to cope with the aftermath of suicide will ever argue that the believing community should sanction it as a favorable way of meeting death. The trauma of dealing with the reality of our own experience that one we loved has, in fact, finally succeeded in that self-destructive action we term suicide, is devastating. We have come face to face with violent death, perhaps even to the point of having discovered the body or having to identify it in the hospital morgue. We have stood beside the grave and heard—as if in another world—the words of the minister. We have come home to an empty house and the sense of desolation has all but overwhelmed us. No wonder that Richard Fox's comment that suicide "is the most significant of all deaths in its impact on the survivors"[8] resonates so strongly with our own personal feelings. We sense within ourselves, the terrible loneliness and despair which drove our loved one to that last desperate act and are horrified by it. But there is still God's grace.

WHEN ROSES WAITED

Among the palest petals,
gathering them for potpourri,
you pushed through brush and thorny tree
to reap the tender rose.

Among the palest petals,
(mostly pink for potpourri),
you mesmerized the thorny tree
and plucked the salted rose.

Another pale, pale summer,
with the light still pink
and the petals free,
but gathering time has ceased to be
for you, my wildest Rose.

CHAPTER TWELVE

A SUMMARY

For the last few chapters we have been examining in some detail those parts of the Bible that deal directly with suicide, as well as the ideas of some of the more influential theologians in the history of the Jewish and Christian communities. It is sometimes difficult to keep so many strands of an argument clearly in mind, so it may be helpful at this point to summarize the evidence:

(1) Nowhere in the Bible, either Old Testament or New Testament is the act or attempt of suicide explicitly condemned. There are several suicides recorded in Scripture, and without exception they are treated just as any other death. The victim is given a normal burial, mourning, at least for some of them, is recorded, and there is no stigma attached to the act itself.

(2) In the Jewish literature of the time between 200 B.C. and A.D. 100 there are records of several suicides. Some of these are individuals (e.g. Razis in 2 Maccabees 14:37-46), others are of larger groups (e.g. the mother and her seven martyred sons in 4 Maccabees 8–18, the Galilean battalion that Josephus commanded, or the Zealots at Masada.[1]) In these contexts there is a recognition that life is from God and ought not to be cast away lightly. Josephus, however, argues that there are occasions where it is a greater sin to commit

idolatry, incest, adultery, or murder, or allow oneself or one's family to be taken prisoner and tortured than it is to commit suicide. It should be noted here that the Jewish community distinguished murder from suicide. Even in the Jewish Talmud, dated somewhere about A.D. 500, there is no explicit forbidding of suicide. There is some brief treatment of the topic in the *Genesis Rabbah*[2] in the discussion of Genesis 9:5-6:

> For your lifeblood I will surely require a reckoning; of every beast I will require it and of man; of every man's brother I will require the life of a man. Whoever sheds the blood of a man, by man shall his blood be shed; for God made man in his own image.

But there is no link made with the sixth commandment. There, the issue is on the "shedding of blood" account, and Saul and the three companions of Daniel are specifically identified as "exceptions" to the blood-guilt law.

(3) The early church, after about A.D. 100, developed a theology and practice of martyrdom that reflected a total disdain for physical life, and promulgated the idea that only in a martyr's bloody death could true discipleship be attained and true witness expressed. This attitude was so widespread that at one point the Roman governor told the Christians that if they wanted to die, they should go and cast themselves over the cliffs, rather than to "keep troubling the magistrates to execute them."

(4) The appalling consequences of this "martyr theology" resulted in Saint Augustine appealing to the command "Thou shalt not kill," as expressly prohibiting suicide (i.e. self-sought martyrdom), unless God had given specific "secret instructions" to an individual to perform the act. Augustine's interpretation of this commandment is a radically new departure in both Judaism and Christianity. His attempt to develop this line of argument is without precedent in the

literature, and is impossible to defend. He himself recognized the weakness of his argument by turning immediately to a series of exceptions and explanations that take any force out of his earlier defense.

(5) Aquinas's appeal to "self-love" and "natural law," fails to take into account the reality of the experience of a large number of people, including both the martyrs about whom Augustine was writing and many suicides.

(6) Aquinas's appeal to the "community loss" and the "right of the state" has no biblical support. It is a pagan concept, totally out of place in the Christian community.

(7) Aquinas's only argument which will bear some weight in the case against suicide is the one that life is from God and therefore is his to reclaim. This approach has some validity, even though the biblical texts used for proof are not convincingly applied. In this discussion, one needs to be careful, though, not to argue that suicide ("self-murder") is outside of God's will for the individual, but murder by another hand is God's will for that person. For if the latter was true, it would mean that punishing a murderer is punishing him for carrying out God's will for the murdered individual.

The evidence, then, is that there is neither valid biblical nor "natural" grounds for the church's condemnation of suicide as an unforgivable sin. It is an act that we do not want to condone or encourage, yet there is no evidence that it brings eternal damnation to its successful practitioners.

And so, whether we are pastoral counselors or family members who, in anguish and sorrow, are trying to put the shattered pieces of our lives back together, we need to recognize the grace of God in his dealings with all of his children. Even Christians can, and do, take their own lives, but even in this situation, God's grace is sufficient.

The twenty-third Psalm reminds us, "Even though I walk through the valley of the shadow of death, I fear no evil; for thou art with me." Some years ago I came across a comment on this verse. I cannot recall who said it, or where I read it, but it has stuck with me, and its truth is real. "The person and power of the Shepherd give the sheep rest even in places of danger." And that is the comfort. Jesus said "My sheep hear my voice, and I know them, and they follow me, and I give them eternal life, and they shall never perish, and no one shall snatch them out of my hand" (John 10:27-28). This is our sustaining hope and our strength. The gospel is the good news that proclaims mercy and grace. The Christ of the gospel is a Christ who knows and understands. He has prepared a place for his own, and has promised us "I will come again and will take you to myself, that where I am you may be also" (John 14:3).

Kate's last note ended "All I ask is Christ's forgiveness and understanding. . . . [I] pray that Jesus will take me . . . [and] I will still be accepted and finally loved for who I am." Her anguish and despair devastated her, and on rereading these words, they devastate me. But there is still God's grace. In the eloquent prayer of Canon J. W. Poole of Coventry Cathedral:

> Remember, O Lord, in thy compassion
> those whose courage fails them
> in the moment of despair;
> when they begin to lose heart,
> renew their hope;
> when they are beaten to the ground,
> raise them up again;
> if they die by their own hand
> forgive them, and forgive us all;
> and assure them, both of thy love
> and of their own worth;
> through our Redeemer Jesus Christ.[3]
>
> Amen.

NOT LOST

I loved you, Kate,
and when you died
thought love would die
in me as well,
that my own shrivelling arms
would unlearn an embrace,
and that my smile
would never find
new boundaries to cross.

But I surprised myself.

Finding someone crying,
my lips remembered
and they smiled.
These arms rushed out
unbidden,
and love leapt strong and wild.

CHAPTER THIRTEEN

"WE'VE BEEN THERE, TOO"

One of the most helpful and encouraging things for us was coming to the sudden realization that we were not alone. The common perception is that Christians don't commit suicide and that Christian families are spared this particular sorrow. But this is not the case. It was incredibly comforting to know that many of our Christian brothers and sisters have "been there, too." Even within the relatively small academic community in which we serve, there were nearly two dozen people who, within the first couple of weeks after Kate's death, told me of cases of suicide within their own families—of a brother, an uncle, a sister, a niece, a parent, or close friend, or relative whose life had ended this way. I suddenly discovered that people I had known for years, and who, by my observation, had lived sheltered, untouched lives, had in fact faced the same loss we were struggling with.

At the same time I was appalled. Why had no one told us? Why had no one shared? Why do we want to hush up the event, bury the scandal, deny the reality, and torture ourselves for years? Is it because we believe we are the only (or at least the very rare) Christian family that has had a suicide? Are we still trapped in the "unforgivable sin" mentality? Are we still caught up in the false theology that if we have enough faith we will never have the problems that our less believing brothers and sisters have? Do we actually believe, deep down, that bad things really don't happen to good (*truly* spirit-filled) people? To admit to the reality of sickness and suffering seems to many Christians to be a denial of the deliverance the gospel seems to promise. Of course, we don't want to go around proclaiming to all the world, "We had a suicide in our family!" We want to keep it quiet, to try to forget, to resume normal life and normal relationships with the stigma buried. But it doesn't happen that way.

One afternoon in the late spring a few months after Kate's death, as I was going from my office to the parking lot behind the building, I met a friend and colleague of many years. We chatted as we walked toward our cars. She asked how things were with us and the family. I told her as best I could, and then in response to other questions, described something of our feelings. At that point she made a comment that reinforced Pastor Jim's urging to "write something." Those comments triggered the first faint plans that culminated in this book. "One of the most important things for us," she said, "is the way you and Gwen have been so open about what happened. The fact that you have been willing to talk about the whole affair without embarrassment has made it easier for us to respond. We know you are still grieving, but that it is being worked through." Then she told me of one of her relatives who, after a suicide in the family several years before, had refused to talk about it at all, tried to deny the reality, and in so doing, rejected any help in mourning. She still has not resolved the grief process.

The story of Job in the Old Testament is an account of a series of unmitigated disasters. A "blameless and upright man, who feared God, and turned away from evil" (1:1) saw, in rapid sequence, the destruction of his livestock, his cattle, his servants, and his ten children. Then he himself was afflicted with "loathsome sores from the sole of his foot to the crown of his head" (2:7). In physical agony and mental anguish he tore his robe, shaved his head, then fell on the ground and *worshiped* (1:20). The Bible story then goes on to tell how Job's three friends came to "condole with him and comfort him" (2:11). Their way of comforting seems odd to us, because for seven days and nights they "sat with him on the ground . . . and no one spoke a word to him, for they saw that his suffering was very great" (2:13).

It was only at the end of this period that Job spoke, and only after he began the conversation did his friends reply. This story provides the basis for the standard ritual of mourning in the Jewish community. The first part of the mourning period is called the *shivah*, or "seven." There are whole lists of things that are or are not to be done during this weeklong period. One of these is that the one who comes to comfort is not to speak until the mourner himself speaks first. Only then can condolences be given.

In the Christian church we have not adopted this requirement for mourners, but there is an important lesson we can learn from the Jewish practice. As my friend said, when we who are most closely involved take the first step to conversation and openness about the situation it makes it easier for others to respond.

Why are we so reticent to talk about suicide, to admit to ourselves and others that this event has been a part of our lives? I hope by this stage that the Bible stories and other things we have examined in the last few chapters have made it clear that there is no valid biblical ground for the belief that suicide is an unforgivable sin. The belief issue is settled.

But I suspect that there is another, multifaceted, problem still very much in need of attention: the shame, anger, and guilt that flood in upon us and drive us away from the help we so desperately need. We were more fortunate than many because we have a colleague and longtime friend, a Christian psychologist whose area of expertise is in family and marriage counseling, to whom we could turn for professional help.

The whole field of psychological counseling is still regarded with distrust and hesitation by many Christians. The fear of this "treatment" is not as pronounced now as it was a generation ago, but there is still the feeling that if a believer should need professional psychological help, that itself is a sign of lack of faith. After all, mental (by which they usually mean spiritual) problems, are to be dealt with by prayer and Bible study (and fasting, if your particular tradition affirms this as a valid spiritual exercise). To permit emotional problems to grow unresolved is to acknowledge spiritual failure. The argument goes that we need to talk to the pastor, not a psychologist.

I suppose all of us have heard these sorts of things said (and perhaps even said them ourselves). But there is a place for professional counseling. As a Christian community we are gradually becoming aware that there are often deep-seated emotional problems that may be helped with appropriate professional care. Most of us have no problem consulting a medical doctor in case of an accident or illness—or even for our annual check-up. Why then should we hesitate about consulting a trained specialist when mental illnesses occur, or when we sense the need to check up on our emotional storms? For some, to admit to the need for this sort of help is almost as devastating as admitting to the fact of the suicide itself. Nevertheless, for us, the decision to seek such help was an important one.

Our counselor friend was more than just a listening ear. He helped us recognize and acknowledge things we already knew intellectually but had difficulty accepting emotionally. To be reminded again of things we already know does not restore the loss, but it is a necessary step in dealing with the sense of guilt that often falls on the survivors. Our questions were the questions always asked: "What if . . . ? Was there anything else I could have done to prevent it? Where did I fail? Why was I not more aware? Did I take it all seriously enough?" And on and on interminably. We try to convince ourselves that if only we had been more diligent, more loving, more careful, we somehow could have prevented that final successful attempt. But we need to be reminded that we cannot live another's life, that depression and despair are extremely difficult to overcome, that even the best treatment is often insufficient, that apparent progress often simply means more energy is available for the potential suicide to actually carry out the act, and that there are times and circumstances when literally nothing effective can be done to prevent the self-inflicted death. Often even the most diligent efforts of the most highly-trained professionals are not enough to counter the successful suicide of one who is so determined.

Beyond this, however, there is, for some, another disturbing element: the sense of relief that the successful suicide brings to the survivors. That relief is real, even with the mourning and the loss, and that in itself often compounds the guilt. We sense, although we do not always ask ourselves, the question "Is it *right* to be relieved at another's death?" Of course this question is broader than just suicide. It covers many other situations. We looked at that question a few pages back and reached some difficult conclusions. For those who are in profound physical suffering or, as in some of the Bible stories, those in immanent danger of deep humiliation, we frequently see death as a release from pain or disgrace. But even there, our guilt remains, and under that burden we somehow forget that we really cannot live another's life. We can guide, help, listen, understand, and where possible, provide the best medical and psychiatric treatment available, but we cannot, ultimately, take responsibility for another person's decisions or actions.

The apostle Paul asks "who are you to pass judgment on the servant of another? It is before his own master that he stands or falls" (Rom. 14:4). And although the context in which these words were spoken is different from ours, they force us back to the central reality—we are *individually* responsible to God.

A LONG GRIEF

Old wounds often split their seams,
and spill the festering out
from where the healing's certainty
hides a nagging doubt;
from where the shiny covering,
that smooth contented place,
harbors in its hollow
some discontented trace.

CHAPTER FOURTEEN

KEEPING ON

For most of us, work is what we do to earn our pay. Play is what we would do whether we were paid or not. God said to Adam:

> cursed is the ground because of you;
> in toil shall you eat of it all the days of your life;
> thorns and thistles it shall bring forth to you;
> and you shall eat of the plants of the field.
> In the sweat of your face
> you shall eat bread
> till you return to the ground (Gen. 3:17-19).

We have somehow taken these words to mean that prior to the fall Adam and Eve lived lives of total ease. We forget that from the very beginning they were placed in the garden to till the ground and care for it (Gen. 2:15).

Even in Eden, the days were filled with assigned activity: there were fields to plow, seed to sow, crops to harvest, bushes to prune, and flowers to pick for the dining room table. I suppose there was grass to cut, although I don't think there were weeds to pull. God has made us to be "sub-creators" to think his thoughts and do his deeds after him. So day by day we give ourselves to honest work, offering it to God, and in so doing, find fulfillment. An ancient Hebrew book called *The Wisdom of Jesus ben Sirach* (or sometimes called

Ecclesiasticus), written about 180 B.C., describes the daily activity of the workers and craftsmen:

> They keep stable the fabric of the world,
>> and their prayer is in the practice of their trade
> (*Sirach* 38:34).

In the section from which this passage is taken, Sirach argues that the farmer and the artisan have little time to meditate on the law of God, because their work demands their full attention. And while this text is from the Old Testament Apocrypha, and is not Scripture, there is truth here. The concentration our work demands tends to shut out all other thoughts.

So it was with us. Just about the same time as Kate's death a whole set of page proofs of a book arrived from the publisher for me to proofread and correct. Much of the material was very detailed and technical, with lots of Hebrew and Greek words, and numerous cross-references that all needed to be carefully checked for accuracy. Proofreading this sort of material is a demanding task at the best of times, one that takes a great deal of concentrated attention to detail and careful comparison, line by line, with the original. As the deadline for the return of the material was mid-January, the task could not be put off for long.

So, for several hours at a time, in between other activities and the constant grieving, we sat around the kitchen table, red pencils in hand, manuscript pages in several piles and proof pages in several others, and read to each other the contents of paragraph after paragraph. And in the work we found comfort. A word or phrase, in or out of context, would trigger paroxysms of laughter, or release new tears, as page by page we worked through the material. Work itself proved to be a blessing that helped us through those first trying weeks.

Pastor Jim often took one of his vacation weeks right

after Christmas, and I had been scheduled to preach on the first Sunday of the new year, 1984. Now he offered to find someone else if I wanted to be excused. The congregation knew what had happened over the last few weeks. They had been a part of our lives. They would understand, whatever I decided to do. The temptation to back out was strong, but I felt that it would be good for me to go ahead as planned.

For many months the media had been debating what 1984 would bring. The focus of much of the speculation was George Orwell's well-known novel *1984*. In it he describes the tightly controlled police state under the all-seeing eye of "Big Brother" in which all personal liberty and freedom is suppressed in the interests of the party. It is a grim and debilitating picture. Yet much of the technology which Orwell only imagined when the book was first published in 1949 was a reality by the 1980s and the possibility of a *1984* scenario was no longer just a novelist's nightmare.

So both personally for us, and people generally, the new year looked forboding. What was there to say in this situation? Again as at the Saturday memorial service, my mind went back to a portion of Scripture I had memorized years ago: the third chapter of 2 Peter. In this chapter the apostle sets out three very simple truths: (1) God, who created the world, judged it once in the great flood and has promised to judge it again in fire at the end of the age. It is *God*, not man who will write "The End" on the last page of human history (3:1-10). (2) In the light of this certainty, our own lives ought to be of the quality that will speed the day of the new heaven and the new earth where righteousness dwells (3:11-13). (3) But it is not enough just to look for God's intervention in history. The goal specified in point 2 above can be reached by zealous effort to "grow in grace in the knowledge of our Lord" (3:18). So my sermon, "Welcome to 1984," was a word of hope and expectation, not based on experience or personal ideas, but on the clear light of God's promise: "We wait" (3:13).

We wait, but we work. There are meals to prepare and dishes to do, garbage to take out and snow to shovel. There are the dozens of routine, daily tasks that make up the fabric of home, and there are the bigger more demanding aspects of just faithfully doing the jobs we get paid to do. We wonder how we can do it, how we can cope with this day, but by God's grace we put one foot in front of the other and go out as his servants, fulfilling the tasks he has assigned to us for these hours. And in the doing, we find again that his grace is sufficient. We learn anew that "it matters to him about [us]" (1 Pet. 5:7 [literal trans.]).

IN THE THIRD YEAR OF GRIEVING

It's time for you to go.

It's time for me
to turn the knob
and make the exit clear.
Too many days and nights—
and now another year—
I've harbored you
until you owned my space.
Too many words in your defence
have kept the image near.

If I'm to go on living
without this painful doubt,
then I must shut the door
upon your going out.

CHAPTER FIFTEEN

REMEMBERING

D ay by day, week by week, we find ourselves further
and further away from "it." The first few days stretch
into the first few weeks, and the first few weeks into
the first months. The story has been told and retold, the
events lived and relived countless times until gradually we
recognize that it no longer fills all our undirected thoughts.
We discover we are "forgetting." That idea comes with a
shock of guilt. How dare we forget! How can we! Yet we
do. It is not a deliberate pushing under, not a careless disre-
gard of all that has happened; it is simply the God-given way
of coping with grief and loss. Life does go on.

And yet it is not quite that simple. A snatch of song, a certain corner of the street, a particular shrub or flower in the
garden, a dream, a glimpse of a stranger in a crowd, an old
photograph—and all the memories return. And we never
know what will trigger them.

At first there were those evenings out, either alone or
with others. Perhaps it was a concert, a party, a family night
supper at the church, or a quiet dinner at the home of a
friend. But whatever it was, there had been fellowship and
friendly banter and discussion and laughter. For a few hours
life had been normal, until after the drive home through the
winter night to the empty house, and the preparations for
bed, in the quiet darkness there came the sudden flood of

guilt. "We have been out enjoying ourselves and Kate's not here any more. She's dead! How can we?" And together we would remember and weep and try to comfort each other.

It was a couple of days after Christmas. The decorations were mostly gone from the store windows to make room for the January sale displays, but the wreaths and streamers still graced the street lamp poles, and the colored lights strung between them reflected in the puddles of slushy water along the curbs. There were five of us: Gwen, Rob, Josh, my mother, and me. We had been out to dinner at a new Chinese restaurant downtown. The food was all one could desire—hot, fresh, and tasty, and served with Oriental grace. Now, after the close warmth of the dining room the open air felt cold and raw as the falling temperature glazed the sidewalk with new ice. We had a short walk back to where the car was parked.

Josh, as nine-year-olds will do, was skipping on ahead, running and sliding on the slippery pavement. I had my mother's arm to steady her, and Rob, a few steps behind, was doing the same for his mother. We were talking about nothing in particular when suddenly I was devastated again. It had been a simple, almost unconscious look at Josh ahead of us that unmade me. The realization came home to me: Josh would never know what Rob and I were experiencing at that moment—ourselves as adults lending supporting arms to our mothers in a simple walk down a city street. His mother was dead. The memory of that evening haunts me still. . . .

The morning sun was not quite strong enough to warm the sanctuary that April Sunday, but it did cast a glow of lightness on the congregation. The church was full. Extra chairs had been placed at the back, and a dozen or so people were sitting in the unused seats beside the choir. There was a sense of joy and adoration as we worshiped together. During one of the hymns I saw, out of the corner of my eye, a young woman. She was a few rows ahead of me and across the aisle. Her long dark hair came nearly to her waist. My heart skipped. I *knew* it wasn't Kate, but that first glance at the dark green dress and the long black hair recalled her presence in a way that undid me. The memories and the grief were overwhelming, and in the midst of the joy all around me, I had to sit. In the pew I could not hold back the tears. . . .

Three thousand miles away from home that summer our little rented Volkswagen took us through the back roads and tiny villages of England's Severn Valley. I had had to go to Britain on business, and we decided to combine that trip with a short vacation. We had visited friends in Oxford, toured the historic sites associated with the industrial revolution, traveled little-used lanes and byways of rural England, and then found our way to a great house that was renowned for its butterfly garden. A large complex of buildings on the property had been turned into a research center and living sanctuary for the preservation and study of butterflies. We decided we would like to see it.

The path from the parking lot led up a short hill and around a small lake surrounded by groves of trees and well-tended gardens. The day was calm and sunny. The butterfly buildings were on the other side of the lake, and as we came down the path past a group of trees, we suddenly saw the buildings mirrored in the smooth surface of the water. I stopped, framed the picture in the camera viewfinder, and snapped the shutter. I was several yards further along the path before I realized Gwen was not with me. I looked back but could not see her, so I began to retrace my steps. As I passed the place where we had seen the buildings across the lake I found her. Whether it was just that scene or whether it was some hidden memory that triggered it, I don't know, but she had found her way to the edge of the water and was sitting there wracked with sobs. Kate had loved butterflies. . . .

The winter of 1973 had been unusually mild, and on that particular Saturday, the weather had been beautiful: bright and warm—more like late April than mid-February. There was not a trace of snow, the grass showed tinges of new green, and the pine trees that flanked the walk in front of the chapel provided welcome shade from the glare of the early afternoon sun.

Inside, in the quiet simplicity of the chapel, the stucco walls and wooden-beamed ceiling glowed with the reflected brilliance of the reds and greens from the stained-glass windows and the harder yellowed tint from the leaded chandeliers. For many of Kate's family, this was a new experience— their first Protestant wedding, and mixed with the excitement of the day there was a sense of curiosity about the whole celebration. The ceremony, very untraditional as many weddings were in the late '60s and early '70s, had been put together by "the kids" themselves, and the music and readings had been drawn from a wide variety of sources.

When the prelude finished, Rob, Sam, and I entered and stood at the front, waiting for the bride. The music they had chosen for the processional was Pachelbel's haunting and melodic *Canon in D*, and we had rehearsed her entrance carefully so she would arrive at the front just as the final resolving chords began. The timing was right, the service began, ran its course, and I pronounced them husband and wife.

One morning, nearly five years after her death, at the breakfast table in our rented house in England, we sat in tears as we heard on the radio for the second time that week, Pachelbel's *Canon in D*. . . .

Our memories are selective. Psychologists and counselors can help us recall some things long buried, but they cannot control our thoughts. Wounds heal, memories fade, but then a touch, or an unexpected movement, a word, or a glance, and suddenly we are swept away again. Those instances may become fewer and fewer, further and further apart, but until death takes us too, they will not entirely cease.

AND STILL THEY COME

On some small day
when life sits still,
thoughts arrive unbidden,
meddle with the memory,
ruffle what I hoped lay hidden:
rousing sorrow to a storm,
and that small day,
to devastation.

CHAPTER SIXTEEN

EPILOGUE

William Cowper's quaint old hymn is not sung much any more, at least in our circles, but the truth still remains.

God moves in a mysterious way,
His wonders to perform;
He plants His footsteps in the sea,
And rides upon the storm.

Ye fearful saints, fresh courage take;
The clouds ye so much dread
Are big with mercy, and shall break
In blessings on your head.

Judge not the Lord with feeble sense,
But trust Him for his grace;
Behind a frowning providence
He hides a smiling face.

His purposes will ripen fast,
Unfolding every hour:
The bud may have a bitter taste,
But sweet will be the flower.

Blind unbelief is sure to err,
And scan His work in vain:
God is His own interpreter,
And He will make it plain.

About 10:00 one morning in the early spring of 1986, I was trying to get out of my office to pick up some material from the college bookstore across campus. I was anxious to get over and back quickly, for I had a number of things to complete before a full afternoon of classes and committee meetings. But with a steady stream of telephone calls, numerous students stopping in for one or another reason, and a couple of my colleagues in with questions or information, it was well after 11:00 before I finally got to the bookstore.

It was crowded, as usual, but I found what I was after and wandered over to the cashier's desk. As I was waiting, I exchanged greetings with a number of students and chatted briefly with a number of people. Then I heard a woman's voice behind me call my name, "Mr. Carr." The form of address was unusual, at least in that context. Among the faculty and staff from the president to the custodian, we are mostly on a first name basis, and with the students and others it is always "Dr. Carr." I turned around to see a young woman with an armload of books looking at me and smiling. My first reaction was that she must be one of my students from my early years of teaching—the pre-"Doctor" days—but I did not recognize her. She must have seen the question on my face, for she spoke again, still smiling, and gave me her name.

I mentally ran through old class lists, trying to place her, but again I drew a blank. Sheepishly I spoke. "I'm sorry, but I don't remember you."

"I'm not surprised," she said. "You met me just once. In Rob's kitchen, the day of the memorial service for Kate."

And then I remembered.

It had been a bright, but bitterly cold and windy Sunday

afternoon. The chapel in Rosedale cemetery was well filled with friends who mourned with us. Pastor Jim had asked me if I wanted to share in the service, but I didn't have the heart, so I simply sat and listened, staring vacantly through my tears at the bouquet of red roses on the altar.

Most of our friends waited to greet us at the door, but it was too cold to linger long outside, so the group dispersed fairly quickly, and a couple of dozen close friends and family hurried the block and a half to the house.

I didn't know her, but I had noticed her standing by herself in the kitchen, not speaking, just leaning against the refrigerator, lost in thought. I don't know who spoke first, or when, but almost as soon as we began to talk she cut through all the superficialities and asked me point-blank: "Mr. Carr, what happens after death? Will I ever see Kate again?"

Her straightforward query caught me by surprise. I had never expected that question so directly from a total stranger—especially one who was young enough to be my own daughter. But the Scripture admonishes us to be always ready to give a reason for our hope, and so very haltingly I explained to her what I believed to be Kate's faith, that her trust in Jesus had been deep and sincere, and in spite of the events of the last couple of days, I was convinced she had really given her life to Christ. I explained the gospel as simply as I could, talked about the hope of the resurrection, and said "Yes, I expect to see Kate again."

She listened quietly, then when I had finished, told me a bit about herself and her relationships with both Rob and Kate during their high school years, their work together in the drama club, and the love she had for both of them. But then we were interrupted and my attention was diverted elsewhere. Later I shared what had happened with Gwen, and found out from Rob who she was, but I did not see her again.

Now, in the bookstore line it all came back. "Of course, I remember that," I said, "but I didn't recognize you."

"That's all right," she said, "But I've been wanting to thank you for that conversation in the kitchen. It changed my life. I was so upset, but what you said seemed to make sense. I thought a lot about it, and the next February I became a Christian. My husband and I are members of a good church in Gloucester, and I'm teaching Sunday school there. That's why I'm here today, getting these books for the kids in my class."

We never know when and how God works. The shattering presence of violent death, a simple sharing of a word, a mixed-up schedule, a confused morning that keeps one from what must be done, are simply parts of his plan. It is trite to say that good can come out of sorrow and mourning. But it is true. Although the later joy of an unexpected testimony of God's saving grace transmitted through a chance encounter can be seen as his confirmation, it does little to ease the hurt and loss. But that is the way life is in this fallen world.

Sin and sorrow and suffering and death are ever-present realities. We never know around which corner disaster lurks. But God's Word and God's grace still stand sure. Jesus said, "Stop being afraid, I will be with you." And after the storm, "the sun of righteousness shall rise, with healing in his wings" (Mal. 4:2, AV).

The release of this edition of *Fierce Goodbye* in conjunction with the Mennonite Media television special gives us the opportunity to bring the story up to date. Some typographical errors have been corrected, and we have taken the opportunity to change some very obvious British expressions into their more familiar American counterparts. Apart from these relatively minor changes, the text remains as it was originally published. A few additional titles have been added to the Suggestions for Further Reading.

It has been twenty years since the early morning phone call that shattered our world and changed our lives forever. In the intervening years, much has changed, but much has remained the same. Butterflies and Pachelbel's *Canon* can still trigger memories. The first weekend in December, even though it is Advent, still has a bittersweet tang. Time has blurred, but not obliterated the anguish and sorrow.

The book provoked extreme reactions, ranging from anger and rejection to extremely favorable reviews—one reviewer declared it "a strange, and to my mind, a bad book . . . so confused that it will only produce more confusion." Another states "it should never have been published for general and particularly student readership," while a third commented it "could be a key item in the Christian community's reservoir of wisdom. I'd like to see it in all Christian and public libraries." Such are the vagaries of book reviews and reviewers.

We have been privileged to speak frequently on the topic of suicide: in formal settings before large audiences, in small groups, and with individuals, face to face or by letter. This is a ministry we did not seek, but one which God has given us.

The most encouraging element for us has been the many dozens of letters we have received from many parts of the world. Correspondents from all over the U.S. and Canada, the United Kingdom, Africa, Latin America, and Australia have written thanking us for the book. Most of these have encountered suicide in their own families or among their friends, and almost unanimously have indicated that until they found the book they thought they were alone in their grief. They could find no one willing to talk with them about it, and with no one to turn to, they had turned inward, burying their sorrow and struggling to cope with their loss alone.

One of the saddest things that we have observed in our working in this area, is the inability of those coping with suicide to be able to talk openly of their loss, and in many cases, even to admit to it. A few years ago Gwen and I were asked to give a workshop on the *Fierce Goodbye* at the New England Congress, a regional gathering of many thousands of believers from all over the northeast. Our session was scheduled for the last slot on Saturday afternoon. Usually by that time most of the delegates are suffering from information overload, and many have already started home. Because of the lateness of the hour, I expected only a few participants. But much to my surprise, the room was crowded—all seats filled and several people standing. We gave our presentation, then opened up for audience participation. At first there were just the usual questions, but after a few of those, a woman sitting near the back began to speak. Very hesitantly and in an almost inaudible voice she asked, "How can I tell my thirty-year-old son that his father committed suicide twenty-five years ago?" She paused and then said "I have never even been able to say the S-word until just now." For twenty-five years she had been unable to face the reality of what has happened to her husband—and to her.

Nor was she the only one at the workshop who finally

found the freedom to admit the heartbreak and devastation which suicide brings to the survivors. The session was supposed to conclude by 4:15 p.m., but a large number of people wanted to remain for talk and questions. It was after 6:00 p.m. before we finally closed, urged out by the cleaning crew who had to reset the room for another event. What we learned from that afternoon is that there are very many hurting people and many of them have no one with whom to share the heavy burden of guilt, pain, sorrow, and loss.

Life goes on. Rob has remarried. Josh is working in his father's business, and keeping company with a delightful young lady. We are both officially retired now, but retirement does not mean doing nothing. Gwen's poetry continues to be heard. She gives public readings frequently, has published a second volume of her poems, and is in the final stages of preparation for a third. My own schedule is still full: writing projects, regular adult Bible classes at church, teaching an occasional class at the college, as well as ongoing involvement with several associated programs there. God has been good, and life is full.

Our prayer is that this new edition of *Fierce Goodbye* will continue to be useful to those who come face to face with the reality of loved ones in this saddest of all deaths.

—G. Lloyd Carr, September 2003

Prologue

1. Because of the deeply personal nature of this story, and being well aware that other members of the extended families involved have their own stories to tell and their own perspectives on the events, we have attempted to safeguard their privacy as much as possible. We have changed the names of all the people involved except our own and Pastor Hay's, but apart from that, our treatment is as accurate as memory and written records can make it.

Chapter 6

1. *New Catholic Encyclopedia*, vol. 13 (New York: McGraw Hill, 1967), 782.

2. See Appendix, p. 150.

3. Thomas Aquinas, *Summa Theologica* (London: Burns, Oates & Washbourne, 1929), 2.2.64.5.5. See Appendix p. 133.

Chapter 7

1. Josephus, *The Antiquities of the Jews*, trans. by H. St J. Thackery (Cambridge, Mass.: Harvard University Press, 1927), 5.8.12. Extracts in Appendix p. 146.

2. 2 Sanhedrin 11:1-2. Extracts in Appendix, p. 153.

3. See Appendix, p. 152.

Chapter 8

1. Extracts in Appendix, p. 136ff.

2. Augustine, *The City of God: The Works of Aurelius Augustine*, edited and translated by Marcus Dods, vol. 1 (Edinburgh: T. & T. Clark, 1871), sec. 19.

3. Extracts in Appendix, pp. 131-33.

4. *New Catholic Encyclopedia*, vol. 13 (New York: McGraw Hill, 1967), 782.

Chapter 9

1. Extracts in Appendix, p. 143ff.

2. Letter *To the Ephesians*, verse 1 in J. B. Lightfoot, *The Apostolic Fathers: Revised Texts with Short Introductions and English Translations* (London: Macmillan, 1893).

3. *To The Trallians*, verse 4 in ibid.

4. *To The Smyrneans*, verse 4 in ibid.

5. *To The Romans*, verse 2, 4, 5, 7 in ibid.

6. *To The Romans*, verse 4 in ibid.

7. Longer extracts, with Trajan's reply, in Appendix p. 154ff.

8. See Paul Louis Landsberg, *The Moral Problem of Suicide* (London: Rockliff, 1953), 79-80.

Chapter 10

1. Thomas Aquinas, *Summa Theologica* (London: Burns, Oates & Washbourne, 1929), 2.2.64.5. Extracts in Appendix, pp. 133-35.

2. Josephus, *The Jewish War*, trans. by H. St J. Thackery (Cambridge, Mass.: Harvard University Press, 1927), 3.8.5. Extracts in the Appendix, pp. 147-50.

3. John Donne, *Biathanathos (Suicide)* (New York: Garland, 1982 [1644]).

4. Extracts in Appendix, pp. 135-36.

5. Aristotle, *The Nicomachean Ethics*, trans. by H. Rackham (Cambridge, Mass.: Harvard University Press, 1926), 5:11.

Chapter 11

1. Dietrich Bonhoeffer, *Ethics* (London: SCM Press, 1971), 123.

2. Aristotle, *The Nicomachean Ethics*, trans. by H. Rackham (Cambridge, Mass.: Harvard University Press, 1926), 3.6. Extracts in Appendix, pp. 135-36.

3. Paul Louis Landsberg, *The Moral Problem of Suicide* (London: Rockliff, 1953), 76.

4. William Raeper, *George MacDonald,* (Lion, 1987), p. 133.

5. C. S. Lewis, "On Living in an Atomic Age," *Present Concerns* (1986): 73-74.

6. Landsberg, *Moral Problem*, 75.

7. Bonhoeffer, *Ethics,* 122-23.

8. "It is not possible to take a morally neutral stance on suicide, since it is the most significant of all deaths in its impact on survivors causing long-lasting grief and guilt and a high suicide expectancy in spouses, around one thousand times the average according to one study [A. C. Cain, ed., *Survivors of Suicide* (Springfield, Ill.: Thomas, 1972]. J. S. Mill's view of the moral innocence of suicide on the ground that it does not damage the lives of others cannot therefore be sustained. No man, with suicide especially, is an island unto himself, or, more pithily, suicide is the skeleton left by the deceased in the survivor's closet." A. S. Duncan, G. R. Dunstan, and R. B. Welbourn, eds., *Dictionary of Medical Ethics*, [1981] p. 426.

Chapter 12

1. Josephus, *The Jewish War*, trans. by H. St J. Thackery (Cambridge, Mass.: Harvard University Press, 1927), 3.8.7, 7.9.1. Extracts in Appendix pp. 149-50.

2. See Appendix, pp. 151-52.

3. From *The Journey: A Meditation with Words and Music,* Festival Service Book Seven (The Royal School of Church Music, Croydon, 1974), 15.

APPENDIX

Frequent reference was made in chapters 6 through 12 to some of the church fathers and the Greek philosophers. As much of their material is not easily located outside theological or large public libraries it seems useful to reproduce here some extended excerpts from their writings that bear specifically on the question of suicide. Much of this will be of interest chiefly to those who wish to investigate a little more fully the primary sources on which the conclusions in those chapters were based. The sections from the fathers will probably be of more immediate interest, but the theology of martyrdom that developed in the period between Ignatius and Augustine drew very heavily on Greek philosophy, particularly Stoicism. In fact, Stoicism was the most serious challenge, intellectually, to the Christian message in those early centuries, and there are many points at which the Stoics and the Christians were in agreement. Disdain for "earthly life" was one of them. The extensive selections from some of the philosophers are chosen to highlight this perspective.

St. Ambrose, *Concerning Virgins.* **A series of three short books on celibacy written by Ambrose in A.D. 377 to his sister Marcellina who had "taken the veil" in 353.**

[Book 3, chapter 7.]

(32) As I am drawing near the close of my address, you make a good suggestion, holy sister, that I should touch upon what we ought to think of the merits of those who have cast themselves down from a height, or have drowned themselves in a river, lest they should fall into the hands of persecutors, seeing that holy Scripture forbids a Christian to lay hands on himself. And indeed as regards virgins placed in the necessity of preserving their purity, we have a plain answer, seeing there exists an instance of martyrdom.

(33) Saint Pelagia lived formerly at Antioch, being about fifteen years old, a sister of virgins, and a virgin herself. She shut herself up at home at the first sound of persecution, seeing herself surrounded by those who would rob her of her faith and purity, in the absence of her mother and her sisters, without any defense, but all the more filled with God. "What are we to do, unless," says she to herself, "thou, a captive

of virginity, takest thought? I both wish and fear to die, for I meet not death but seek it. Let us die if we are allowed, or if they will not allow it, still let us die. God is not offended by a remedy against evil, and faith permits the act. In truth, if we think of the real meaning of the word, how can what is voluntary be violence? It is rather violence to wish to die and not to be able. And we do not fear any difficulty. For who is there who wishes to die and is not able to do so, when there are so many easy ways to death? For I can now rush upon the sacrilegious altars and overthrow them, and quench with my blood the kindled fires. I am not afraid that my right hand may fail to deliver the blow, or that my breast may shrink from the pain. I shall leave no sin to my flesh. I fear not that a sword may be wanting. I can die by my own weapons, I can die without the help of an executioner, in my mother's bosom."

(34) She is said to have adorned her head, and to have put on a bridal dress, so that one would say she was going to a bridegroom, not to death. But when the hateful persecutors saw that they had lost the prey of her chastity, they began to seek her mother and sisters. But they, by a spiritual flight, already held the field of chastity, when, as on the one side, persecutors suddenly threatened them, and on the other, escape was shut off by an impetuous river, they said, what do we fear? See the water, what hinders us from being baptized? And this is the baptism whereby sins are forgiven, and kingdoms are sought. This is a baptism after which no one sins. Let the water receive us, which is wont to regenerate. Let the water receive us, which makes virgins. Let the water receive us, which opens heaven, protects the weak, hides death, makes martyrs. We pray Thee, God, Creator of all things, let not the water scatter our bodies, deprived of the breath of life; let not death separate our obsequies, whose lives affection has always conjoined; but let our constancy be one, our death one, and our burial also be one.

(35) Having said these words, and having slightly girded up the bosom of their dress, to veil their modesty without impeding their steps, joining hands as though to lead a dance, they went forward to the middle of the river bed, directing their steps to where the stream was more violent, and the depth more abrupt. No one drew back, no one ceased to go on, no one tried where to place her steps, they were anxious only when they felt the ground, grieved when the water was shallow, and glad when it was deep. One could see the pious mother tightening her grasp, rejoicing in her pledges, afraid of a fall lest even the stream should carry off her daughters from her. "These victims, O Christ," said she, "do I offer as leaders of chastity, guides on my journey, and companions of my sufferings."

(37) But who would have cause to wonder that they had such constancy whilst alive, seeing that even when dead they preserved the position of their bodies unmoved? The water did not lay bare their corpses,

nor did the rapid course of the river roll them along. Moreover, the holy mother, though without sensation, still maintained her loving grasp, and held the sacred knot which she had tied, and loosed not her hold in death, that she who had paid her debt to religion might die leaving her piety as her heir. For those whom she had joined together with herself for martyrdom, she claimed even to the tomb.

Thomas Aquinas, *Summa Theologica*, 2.2.64.5.

FIFTH ARTICLE: WHETHER IT IS LAWFUL TO KILL ONESELF?

We proceed thus to the Fifth Article:—

Objection 1. It would seem lawful for a man to kill himself. For murder is a sin in so far as it is contrary to justice. But no man can do an injustice to himself, as is proved in *Ethic.* 5:11. Therefore no man sins by killing himself.

Obj. 2. Further, it is lawful, for one who exercised public authority, to kill evildoers. Now he who exercises public authority is sometimes an evildoer. Therefore he may lawfully kill himself.

Obj. 3. Further, it is lawful for a man to suffer spontaneously a lesser danger that he may avoid a greater: thus it is lawful for a man to cut off a decayed limb even from himself, that he may save his whole body. Now sometimes a man, by killing himself, avoids a greater evil, for example an unhappy life, or the shame of sin. Therefore a man may kill himself.

Obj. 4. Further, Samson killed himself, as related in Judges 16, yet he is numbered among the saints (Heb. 11). Therefore, it is lawful for a man to kill himself.

Obj. 5. Further, it is related (2 Macc. 14:42) that a certain Razias killed himself, *choosing to die nobly rather than to fall into the hands of the wicked, and to suffer abuses unbecoming his noble birth.* Now nothing that is done nobly and bravely is unlawful. Therefore suicide is not unlawful.

On the contrary, Augustine says (*The City of God* 1:20): *Hence it follows that the words 'Thou shalt not kill' refer to the killing of a man;—not another man; therefore not even thyself. For he who kills himself, kills nothing else than a man.*

I answer that, It is altogether unlawful to kill oneself, for three reasons. First, because everything naturally loves itself, the result being that everything naturally keeps itself in being, and resists corruptions sofar as it can. Wherefore suicide is contrary to the inclination of nature, and to charity whereby every man should love himself. Hence suicide is always a mortal sin, as being contrary to the natural law and to charity.

Secondly, because every part, as such, belongs to the whole. Now every man is part of the community, and so, as such, he belongs to the community. Hence, by killing himself, he injures the community as the Philosopher declares (*Ethic.* 5:11).

Thirdly, because life is God's gift to man, and is subject to His power, Who kills and makes to live. Hence whoever takes his own life, sins against God, even as he who kills another's slave, sins against that slave's master, and as he who usurps to himself judgment of a matter not entrusted to him. For it belongs to God alone to pronounce sentence of death and life, according to Deuteronomy 32:39, *I will kill and I will make to live.*

Reply Obj. 1. Murder is a sin, not only because it is contrary to justice, but also because it is opposed to charity which a man should have towards himself: in this respect suicide is a sin in relation to oneself. In relation to the community and to God, it is sinful, by reason also of its opposition to justice.

Reply Obj. 2. One who exercises public authority may lawfully put to death an evildoer, since he can pass judgment on him. But no man is judge of himself. Wherefore it is not lawful for one who exercises public authority to put himself to death for any sin whatever: although he may lawfully commit himself to the judgment of others.

Reply Obj. 3. Man is made master of himself through his free-will: wherefore he can lawfully dispose of himself as to those matters which pertain to this life which is ruled by man's free-will. But the passage from this life to another and happier one is subject not to man's free-will, but to the power of God. Hence it is not lawful for a man to take his own life that he may pass to a happier life, nor that he may escape any unhappiness whatsoever of the present life, because the ultimate and most fearsome evil of this life is death, as the Philosopher states (*Ethic.* 3:6). Therefore to bring death upon oneself in order to escape the other afflictions of this life, is to adopt a greater evil in order to avoid a lesser. In like manner, it is unlawful to take one's own life on account of one's having committed a sin, both because by so doing one does oneself a very great injury, by depriving oneself of the time needful for repentance, and because it is not lawful to slay an evildoer except by the sentence of the public authority. Again it is unlawful for a woman to kill herself lest she be violated, because she ought not to commit on herself the very great sin of suicide to avoid the lesser sin of another. For she commits no sin in being violated by force, provided she does not consent, *since without consent of the mind there is no stain on the body*, as the Blessed Lucy declared. Now it is evident that fornication and adultery are less grievous sins than taking a man's, especially one's own, life: since the latter is most grievous, because one injures oneself, to whom one owes the greatest love. Moreover, it is most dangerous since no time is left wherein to expiate it by repentance. Again it is not lawful for anyone to take his own life for fear he should consent to sin, because *evil must not be done that good may come* (Rom. 3:8) or that evil may be avoided, especially if the evil be of small account and an uncertain event, for it is uncertain whether one will at some future time consent to a sin, since God is able to deliver man from sin under any temptation whatever.

Reply Obj. 4. As Augustine says (*The City of God,* 1:21), *not even Samson is to be excused that he crushed himself together with his enemies under the ruins of the house, except the Holy Ghost, Who had wrought many wonders through him, had secretly commanded him to do this.* He assigns the same reason in the case of certain holy women, who at the time of persecution took their own lives, and who are commemorated by the Church.

Reply Obj. 5. It belongs to fortitude that a man does not shrink from being slain by another, for the sake of the good of virtue, and that he may avoid sin. But that a man take his own life in order to avoid penal evils has indeed an appearance of fortitude (for which reason some, among whom was Razias, have killed themselves thinking to act from fortitude), yet it is not true fortitude, but rather a weakness of soul unable to bear penal evils, as the Philosopher (*Ethic.* 3:7) and Augustine (*The City of God* 1:22-23) declare.

Aristotle, *Nicomachean Ethics* **(trans. H. Rackham). *Nicomacus was Aristotle's son who was killed in battle as a young man.***

[Book 5, section 11:1-3]
The foregoing discussion has indicated the answer to the question, Is it possible or not for a man to commit injustice against himself? One class of just actions consists of those acts, in accordance with any virtue, which are ordained by law. For instance, the law does not sanction suicide (and what it does not expressly sanction, it forbids). Further, when a man voluntarily (which means with knowledge of the person affected and the instrument employed) does an injury (not in retaliation) that is against the law, he commits injustice. But he who kills himself in a fit of passion, voluntarily does an injury (against the right principle [of "retaliation"]) which the law does not allow. Therefore the suicide commits injustice; but against whom? It seems to be against the state rather than against himself; for he suffers voluntarily, and nobody suffers injustice voluntarily. This is why the state exacts a penalty; a suicide is punished by certain marks of dishonor, as being an offence against the state.

[Book 3, Section 6. This is a discussion of "Courage," which Aristotle identifies as the "First Virtue."]
What then are the fearful things in respect of which Courage is

displayed? I suppose those which are the greatest, since there is no one more brave in enduring danger than the courageous man. Now the most terrible thing of all is death; for it is the end, and when a man is dead, nothing, we think, either good or evil can befall him any more.

[Book 3, Section 7:2, 13]

(2) . . . the courageous man . . . although he will sometimes fear even terror not beyond man's endurance, he will do so in the right way, and he will endure them as principle dictates, for the sake of what is noble; for that is the end at which virtue aims.

(13) Courage is the observance of the mean in relation to things that inspire confidence or fear, in the circumstances stated; and it is confidence that endures because it is noble to do so or base not to do so. But to seek death in order to escape from poverty, or the pangs of love, or from pain or sorrow, is not the act of a courageous man, but rather of a coward; for it is weakness to fly from troubles, and the suicide does not endure death because it is noble to do so, but to escape evil.

Augustine, *The City of God.*

[Book 1, section 11]

But, it is added, many Christians were slaughtered, and were put to death in a hideous variety of cruel ways. Well, if this be hard to bear, it is assuredly the common lot of all who are born into this life. Of this at least I am certain, that no one has ever died who was not destined to die some time. Now the end of life puts the longest life on a par with the shortest. . . . That death is not to be judged an evil which is the end of a good life; for death becomes evil only by the retribution which follows it. They, then, who are destined to die, need not be careful to inquire what death they are to die, but into what place death will usher them. And since Christians are well aware that the death of the godly pauper whose sores the dogs licked was far better than of the wicked rich man who lay in purple and fine linen, what harm could these terrific deaths do to the dead who had lived well?

[Book 1, section 16-17]

(16) . . . let this, therefore, in the first place, be laid down as an unassailable position, that the virtue which makes the life good has its throne in the soul, and thence rules the members of the body, which becomes holy in virtue of the holiness of the will; and that while the will remains firm and unshaken, nothing that another person does with the body, or upon the body, is any fault of the person who suffers it, so long as he cannot escape it without sin. But as not only pain may be inflicted, but lust gratified on the body of another, whenever anything

of this latter kind takes place, shame invades even a thoroughly pure spirit from which modesty has not departed—shame, lest that act which could not be suffered without some sensual pleasure, should be believed to have been committed also with some assent of the will.

(17) And consequently, even if some of these virgins killed themselves to avoid such disgrace, who that has any human feeling would refuse to forgive them? And as for those who would not put an end to their lives, lest they might seem to escape the crime of another by a sin of their own, he who lays this to their charge as a great wickedness is himself not guiltless of the fault of folly. For if it is not lawful to take the law into our own hands, and slay even a guilty person, whose death no public sentence has warranted, then certainly he who kills himself is a homicide, and so much the guiltier of his own death, as he was more innocent of that offence for which he doomed himself to die. Do we justly execrate the deed of Judas, and does truth itself pronounce that by hanging himself he rather aggravated than expiated the guilt of that most iniquitous betrayal, since, by despairing of God's mercy in his sorrow that wrought death, he left to himself no place for a healing penitence? How much more ought he to abstain from laying violent hands on himself who has done nothing worthy of such a punishment! For Judas, when he killed himself, killed a wicked man; but he passed from this life chargeable not only with the death of Christ, but with his own: for though he killed himself on account of his crime, his killing himself was another crime. Why, then, should a man who has done no ill do ill to himself, and by killing himself kill the innocent to escape another's guilty act, and perpetrate upon himself a sin of his own, that the sin of another may not be perpetrated on him?

[Book 1, section 18]
. . . let us rather draw this conclusion, that while the sanctity of the soul remains even when the body is violated, the sanctity of the body is not lost; and that, in like manner, the sanctity of the body is lost when the sanctity of the soul is violated, though the body itself remain intact. And therefore a woman who has been violated by the sin of another, and without any consent of her own, has no cause to put herself to death; much less has she cause to commit suicide in order to avoid such violation, for in that case she commits certain homicide to prevent a crime which is uncertain as yet, and not her own.

[Book 1, sections 20-22]
(20) It is not without significance, that in no passage of the holy canonical books there can be found either divine precept or permission to take away our own life, whether for the sake of entering on the enjoyment of immortality, or of shunning, or ridding ourselves of anything whatever. Nay, the law, rightly interpreted, even prohibits suicide,

where it says, "Thou shalt not kill." This is proved specially by the omission of the words "thy neighbor," which are inserted when false witness is forbidden: "Thou shalt not bear false witness against thy neighbor. . . ." How much greater reason have we to understand that a man may not kill himself, since in the commandment "Thou shalt not kill" there is no limitation added, nor any exception made in favor of anyone, and least of all in favor of him on whom the command is laid! . . . The commandment is "Thou shalt not kill man," therefore neither another nor yourself, for he who kills himself still kills nothing else than a man.

(21) However, there are some exceptions made by the divine authority to its own law, that men may not be put to death. These exceptions are of two kinds, being justified either by a general law, or by a special commission granted for a time to some individual. And in this latter case, he to whom authority is delegated, and who is but the sword in the hand of him who uses it, is not himself responsible for the death he deals. And, accordingly, they who have waged war in obedience to the divine command, or in conformity with His laws have represented in their persons the public justice or the wisdom of government, and in this capacity have put to death wicked men; such persons have by no means violated the commandment, "Thou shalt not kill." Abraham indeed was not merely deemed guiltless of cruelty, but was even applauded for his piety, because he was ready to slay his son in obedience to God, not to his own passion. And it is reasonably enough made a question, whether we are to esteem it to have been in compliance with a command of God that Jephthah killed his daughter, because she met him when he had vowed that he would sacrifice to God whatever first met him as he returned victorious from battle. Samson, too, who drew down the house on himself and his foes together, is justified only on this ground, that the Spirit who wrought wonders by him had given him secret instructions to do this. With the exception, then, of these two classes of cases, which are justified either by a just law that applies generally, or by a special intimation from God Himself, the fountain of all justice, whoever kills a man, either himself or another, is implicated in the guilt of murder.

(22) But they who have laid violent hands on themselves are perhaps to be admired for their greatness of soul, though they cannot be applauded for the soundness of their judgment. However, if you look at the matter more closely, you will scarcely call it greatness of soul, which prompts a man to kill himself rather than bear up against some hardships of fortune, or sins in which he is not implicated. . . .

Again, it is said many have killed themselves to prevent an enemy doing so. But we are not inquiring whether it has been done, but whether it ought to have been done. Sound judgment is to be preferred even to examples, and indeed examples harmonize with the voice of reason;

but not all examples, but those only which are distinguished by their piety, and are proportionately worthy of imitation. For suicide we cannot cite the examples of patriarchs, prophets, or apostles; though our Lord Jesus Christ, when He admonished them to flee from city to city if they were persecuted, might very well have taken that occasion to advise them to lay violent hands on themselves, and so escape their persecutors. But seeing He did not do this, nor proposed this mode of departing this life, though He were addressing His own friends for whom He had promised to prepare everlasting mansions, it is obvious that such examples as are produced from "the nations that forget God," give no warrant of imitation to the worshippers of the one true God.

[Book 1, section 25]

But, we are told, there is ground to fear that, when the body is subjected to the enemy's lust, the insidious pleasure of sense may entice the soul to consent to the sin, and steps must be taken to prevent so disastrous a result. And is not suicide the proper mode of preventing not only the enemy's sin, but the sin of the Christian so allured? Now, in the first place, the soul which is lead by God and His wisdom, rather than by bodily concupiscence, will certainly never consent to the desire aroused in its own flesh by another's lust. And, at all events, if it be true, as the truth plainly declares, that suicide is a detestable and damnable wickedness, who is such a fool as to say, Let us sin now, that we may obviate a possible future sin; let us now commit murder, lest we perhaps afterwards should commit adultery? If we are so controlled by iniquity that innocence is out of the question, and we can at best but make a choice of sins, is not a future and uncertain adultery preferable to a present and certain murder? Is it not better to commit a wickedness which penitence may heal, than a crime which leaves no place for healing contrition?

[Book 1, section 26]

But, they say, in the time of persecution, some holy women escaped those who menaced them with outrage, by casting themselves into rivers which they knew would drown them; and having died in this manner, they are venerated in the church catholic as martyrs. Of such persons I do not presume to speak rashly. I cannot tell whether there may not have been vouchsafed to the church some divine authority, proved by trustworthy evidences, for so honoring their memory: it may be that it is so. It may be they were not deceived by human judgment, but prompted by divine wisdom, to their act of self-destruction. We know that this was the case with Samson. And when God enjoins any act, and intimates by plain evidence that He has enjoined it, who will call obedience criminal? Who will accuse so religious a submission? But then every man is not justified in sacrificing his son to God, because Abraham was commendable in so doing. The soldier who has slain a man in obedience to the authority under which he is lawfully commissioned, is not accused of murder by any law of his state; nay, if he has not slain him, it is then he is accused of treason to the state, and of despising the law. But if he has been acting on his own authority, and at his own impulse, he has in this case incurred the crime of shedding human blood. And thus he is punished for doing without orders the very thing he is punished for neglecting to do when he has been ordered. If the commands of a general make so great a difference, shall the commands of God make none? He, then, who knows it is unlawful to kill himself, may nevertheless do so if he is ordered by Him whose commands we may not neglect. Only let him be very sure that the divine command has been signified. As for us, we can become privy to the secrets of conscience only in so far as these are disclosed to us, and so far only do we judge: "No one knoweth the things of a man, save the spirit of man which is in him." But this we affirm, this we maintain, this we every way pronounce to be right, that no man ought to inflict on himself voluntary death, for this is to escape the ills of time by plunging into those of eternity; that no man ought to do so on account of another man's sins; for this were to escape a guilt which could not pollute him, by incurring great guilt of his own; that no man ought to do so on account of his own past sins, for he has all the more need of this life that these sins may be healed by repentance; that no man should put an end to this life to obtain that better life we look for after death, for those who die by their own hand have no better life after death.

[Book 1, section 27]
There remains one reason for suicide which I mentioned before, and which is thought a sound one—namely, to prevent one's falling into sin either through the blandishments of pleasure or the violence of pain. If this reason were a good one, then we should be impelled to exhort men at once to destroy themselves, as soon as they have been washed in the laver of regeneration, and have received the forgiveness of all sin. Then is the time to escape all future sin, when all past sin is blotted out. And if this escape be lawfully secured by suicide, why not then specially? Why does any baptized person hold his hand from taking his own life? . . . If any one thinks that such persuasion should be attempted, I say not he is foolish, but mad. With what face, then, can he say to any man, "Kill yourself, lest to your small sins you add a heinous sin, while you live under an unchaste master, whose conduct is that of a barbarian?" How can he say this, if he cannot without wickedness say, "Kill yourself, now that you are washed from all your sins, lest you fall again into similar or even aggravated sins, while you live in a world which has such power to allure by its unclean pleasures,

to torment by its terrible cruelties, to overcome by its errors and terrors?" It is wicked to say this; it is therefore wicked to kill oneself. For if there could be any just cause of suicide, this were so. And since not even this is so, there is none.

Epictetus, *The Discourses (trans. W. A. Oldfather). Epictetus was a leading Stoic philosopher who lived from A.D. 50 to 130. He was a little younger than Josephus, and a contemporary of Ignatius. The* Discourses *were written down by Arrian, one of Epictetus's disciples. While many of the Stoics defended the practice of suicide, Epictetus did not. The following excerpts from the* Discourses *are the major ones where this topic is addressed.*

[Book 1, chapter 9]
I . . . ought not to be sitting here devising how to keep you from thinking too meanly of yourselves; [I] should rather be striving to prevent there being among you any young men of such a sort that, when once they have realized their kinship to the gods and we have these fetters as it were fastened upon us—the body and its passions, and whatever things on their account are necessary to us for the management of life, and our tarrying therein—they may desire to throw aside all these things as burdensome and vexatious and unprofitable and depart to their kindred. . . . You, for your part, would come to him saying: "Epictetus, we can no longer endure to be imprisoned in this paltry body, giving it food and drink, and resting and cleansing it, and, to crown all, being on its account brought into contact with these people and those. Are not these things indifferent—indeed, nothing—to us? And is not death no evil? And are we not in a manner akin to God, and have we not come from him? Suffer us to go back whence we came; suffer us to be freed at last from these fetters that are fastened to us and weigh us down. . . ." And thereupon it were my part to say: "Men, wait upon God. When He shall give the signal and set you free from this service, then shall you depart to Him; but for the present endure to abide in this place, where he has stationed you. Short indeed is the time of your abiding here, and easy to bear for men of your convictions."

[Book 1, chapter 24]
But to sum it all up: remember that the door has been thrown open. Do not become a greater coward than the children, but just as they say "I won't play any longer" when the thing does not please them, so do you also, when things seem to you to have reached that stage, merely say "I won't play any longer" and take your departure; but if you stay, stop lamenting.

[Book 3, chapter 24]

Do you tell me that any word is ill-omened which signifies some process of nature? Say that also the harvesting of ears of grain is ill-omened, for it signifies the destruction of the ears; but not of the universe. Say that also for leaves to fall is ill-omened, and for the fresh fig to turn into a dried fig, and a cluster of grapes to turn into raisins. For all these things are changes of a preliminary state into something else; it is not a case of destruction, but a certain ordered dispensation and management. This is what going abroad means, a slight change; this is the meaning of death, a greater change of that which now is, not into what is not, but into what is not *now.*—Shall I, then, be no more?—No, you will not be, but something else will be, something different from that of which the universe now had need. And this is but reasonable, for you came into being, not when *you* wanted, but when the universe had need of you.

. . . the good and excellent man . . . has come . . . with due obedience to God. "Is it Thy will that I should still remain? I will remain as a free man, as a noble man, as Thou didst wish it; for Thou hast made me free from hindrance in what was mine own. And now hast Thou no further need of me? Be it well with Thee. I have been waiting here until now because of Thee and of none other, and now I obey Thee and depart. . . ." If thou sendest me to a place where men have no means of living in accordance with nature, I shall depart this life, not in disobedience to Thee, but as though Thou wert sounding for me the recall. [Note: another, slightly freer translation of this sentence is "Hence the man who finds it no longer possible to obey God, or in other words to live as his nature requires, is to perceive precisely in this fact an intimation from God that it is time to depart from life."] I do not abandon Thee—far be that from me! but I perceive that Thou hast no need of me. Yet if there be vouchsafed a means of living in accordance with nature, I will seek no other place than that in which I am, or other men than those who are now my associates."

Have thoughts like these ready at hand by night and by day; write them, read them, make your conversation about them, communing with yourself, or saying to another, "Can you give me some help in this matter?" And again, go now to one man and now to another. Then, if some one of those things happens which are called undesirable, immediately the thought that it was not unexpected will be the first thing to lighten the burden. For in every case it is a great help to be able to say, "I knew that the son whom I had begotten was mortal."

[Book 4, chapter 1]

Study these things, these judgments, these arguments, look at these examples, if you wish to be free. . . . For the sake of what is called freedom some men hang themselves, others leap over precipices, sometimes whole cities perish; for true freedom, which cannot be plotted against and is secure, will you not yield up to God at His demand, what He has given?

Ignatius *(trans. J. B. Lightfoot in* The Apostolic Fathers*). In the seven epistles of Ignatius there are numerous references to martyrdom. The most important of these are given here. Six of the seven letters are to churches in Asia Minor (modern Turkey), the seventh is a personal letter to Polycarp, the bishop of the church at Smyrna. The epistles are listed here in the generally accepted chronological order.*

[To the Ephesians]
(1) . . . I . . . was hoping through your prayers to succeed in fighting with the wild beasts in Rome, that by so succeeding I might have power to be a disciple.

[To the Magnesians]
(14) Remember me in your prayers that I may attain unto God.

[To the Trallians]
(4) For though I desire to suffer, yet I know not whether I am worthy: for the envy of the devil is unseen indeed by many, but against me it wages the fiercer war. So then I crave gentleness, whereby the prince of this world is brought to nought.

(10) But if it were as certain persons who are godless, that is unbelievers, say that He [Christ] suffered only in semblance [this was a part of the theology of the Docetic sects], being themselves mere semblance, why am I in bonds? And why do I also desire to fight with wild beasts? So I die in vain. Truly then I lie against the Lord.

(12) . . . for my bonds exhort you, which for Jesus Christ's sake I bear about, entreating that I may attain unto God. . . . And pray ye also for me who have need of your love in the mercy of God, that I may be vouchsafed the lot I am eager to attain, to the end that I be not found reprobate.

(13) . . . my spirit is offered up for you, not only now, but also when I shall attain unto God.

[To the Romans]
(1) . . . in answer to my prayer . . . for wearing bonds in Jesus Christ I hope to salute you, if it should be the Divine will that I should be counted worthy to reach unto the end; for the beginning verily is well ordered, if so be I shall attain unto the goal, that I may receive mine inheritance without hindrance . . . for me it is most difficult to attain unto God, unless ye shall spare me.

(2) . . . for neither shall I myself ever find an opportunity such as this

to attain unto God, nor can ye, if ye be silent, win the credit of any nobler work. . . . Nay, grant me nothing more than that I be poured out a libation to God, while there is still an altar ready. . . . It is good to set from the world unto God, that I may rise unto Him.

(4) I write to all the churches, as I bid all men know, that of my own free will I die for God, unless ye should hinder me. . . . Let me be given to the wild beasts, for through them I can attain unto God. I am God's wheat, and I am ground by the teeth of wild beasts that I may be found pure bread [of Christ]. Rather entice the wild beasts that they may become my sepulchre and may leave no part of my body behind, so that I may not, when I am fallen asleep, be burdensome to anyone. Then shall I be truly a disciple of Jesus Christ when the world shall not so much as see my body. Supplicate the Lord for me, that through these instruments, I may be found a sacrifice to God. . . . Yet if I shall suffer, then am I a freed-man of Jesus Christ, and I shall rise free in Him. . . .

(5) From Syria even unto Rome I fight with wild beasts, by land and sea, by night and by day, being bound amidst ten leopards, even a company of soldiers who only wax worse when they are kindly treated. Howbeit through their wrong doings I become more completely a disciple; yet I am not hereby justified. May I have joy of the beasts that have been prepared for me; and I pray that I may find them prompt; nay I will entice them that they may devour me promptly, not as they have done to some, refusing to touch them through fear. Yea though of themselves they should not be willing while I am ready, I myself will force them to it. . . . Now I am beginning to be a disciple. . . . May naught of things visible and things invisible envy me; that I may attain unto Jesus Christ. Come fire and cross and grapplings with wild beasts [cuttings and manglings], wrenching of bones, hacking of limbs, crushings of my whole body, come cruel tortures of the devil to assail me. Only be it mine to attain unto Jesus Christ

(6) . . . it is good for me to die for Jesus Christ rather than to reign over the farthest bounds of earth. . . . The pangs of a new birth are upon me. . . . Do not hinder me from living, do not desire my death. Bestow not on the world one who desireth to be God's. . . . Suffer me to receive the pure light. When I am come thither, then shall I be a man. Permit me to be an imitator of the passion of my God. . . .

(7) . . . [for] I write to you in the midst of life, yet lusting after death. My lust hath been crucified and there is no fire of material longing in me but only water living and speaking in me saying within me, 'Come to the Father'. . . .

(8) I desire no longer to live after the manner of men.

[To the Philadelphians]
(5) I watch over your safety; yet not I, but Jesus Christ, wearing whose bonds I am the more afraid, because I am not yet perfected. But

your prayer will make me perfect [unto God], that I may attain unto the inheritance wherein I have found mercy.

[To the Smyrnaeans]
(4) For if these things were done by our Lord in semblance, then I am also a prisoner in semblance. And why then have I delivered myself over to death, unto fire, unto sword, unto wild beasts? But near to the sword, near to God; in company with wild beasts, in company with God. Only let it be in the name of Jesus Christ, so that we may suffer together with Him.

(11) . . . the church . . . in Antioch . . . whence coming a prisoner in most godly bonds, I salute all men, though I am not worthy to belong to it, being the very last of them. By the Divine will was this vouchsafed to me, not of my own complicity, but by God's grace, which I pray may be given to me perfectly, that through your prayers I may attain unto God.

[To Polycarp, (A.D. 69-155), Bishop of Smyrna for nearly sixty years. He himself was a martyr.]
(7) . . . if so be I may through suffering attain unto God, that I may be found a disciple through your intercession.

Josephus. *Josephus was a Jewish military leader who was active in the revolt against Rome in the third quarter of the first century A.D. The* Antiquities of the Jews *is his re-telling of the Old Testament stories, and of the events of what we call the inter-testamental period, that is the years between the end of the Old Testament and the beginning of the New. These excerpts are Josephus's treatment of the Old Testament suicides discussed more fully in Chapter 10, above. Josephus's words are important as they also reflect the silence of Scripture on the question of suicide. There is considerable variation in the way names of people and places are transcribed into English here, but there is little difficulty in identifying them correctly.*

[Antiquities 5:7:5, on Abimelech]
. . . as he came rushing close beside the gates, a woman hurled a fragment of a millstone and struck him on the head. Prostrated to earth, Abimelech besought his armor-bearer to slay him, lest his death should be deemed the work of a woman; and he obeyed his behest. Such was the penalty paid by Abimelech for the crime he had perpetrated on his brothers and for his outrageous treatment of the Shechemites; and the fate which befell these last fulfilled the prediction of Jotham.

[Antiquities 5:8:12, on Samson]

But in the course of time Samson's locks grew; and once when the Philistines were keeping a public festival and their lords and chief notables were feasting together in one place—a hall with two columns supporting its roof—Samson at their summons was led to the banquet, that they might mock him over their cups. And he, deeming it direr than all his ills to be unable to be avenged of such insults, induced the boy who led him by the hand—telling him that from weariness he needed a stay whereon to rest—to conduct him close to the columns. And when he was come thither, flinging all his weight upon them, he brought down the hall, overturning the columns upon three thousand men who all perished, and among them Samson. Such was his end, after governing Israel for twenty years. And it is but right to admire the man for his valor, his strength, and the grandeur of his end, as also for the wrath which he cherished to the last against his enemies. That he let himself be ensnared by a woman must be imputed to human nature which succumbs to sins; but testimony is due to him for his surpassing excellence in all the rest.

[Antiquities 6:14:6-8, on Saul]

When these [Saul's three sons] fell, the Hebrew host took flight, disorder and confusion ensued, and there was a massacre as the enemy fell upon them. But Saul fled, having the ablest men around him; of these, when the Philistines sent javelin-throwers and archers after him, he lost all but a few. He himself, after fighting magnificently and receiving numerous wounds, until he could no longer hold out nor endure under these blows, was too weak to kill himself and bade his armor-bearer draw his sword and thrust it through him before the enemy should take him alive. But as the armor-bearer did not dare to slay his master, Saul drew his own sword himself, and, fixing it with its point toward him, sought to fling himself upon it, but was unable either to push it in or, by leaning upon it, to drive the weapon home. Then he turned and seeing a youth standing there, asked him who he was, and on learning that he was an Amalekite, begged him to force the sword in, since he could not do this with his own hands, and so procure him such a death as he desired. This he did, and after stripping off the bracelet of gold on Saul's arm and his royal crown, disappeared. Then the armor-bearer, seeing that Saul was dead, killed himself; and of the king's bodyguard, not a man escaped, but all fell on that mountain called Gelboue. . . . But when the inhabitants of Jabis in the region of Galaditis heard that they [the Philistines] had mutilated the corpses of Saul and his sons, they were horrified at the thought of leaving them unburied, and so the most valiant and hardy among them—and this city breeds men stalwart of body and soul—set forth, and having marched all night, reached Bethsan. Then having advanced to the enemy's ramparts and taken down the bodies of Saul and his sons, they bore them to Jabesa, and the enemy was neither able nor dared to hinder them, because of their prowess. The Jabesenians with public mourning buried their bodies in the fairest spot in their country called Arouna ("Plowland") and with their wives and children continued for seven days to mourn for them, beating the breast and bewailing the king and his sons, without touching either meat or drink. To such an end did Saul come, as Samuel had predicted, because he had disobeyed God's commandments touching the Amalekites, and because he had destroyed the family of Abimelek the high priest and Abimelek himself and the city of the high priests. He reigned eighteen years during the lifetime of Samuel and for twenty-two years more after the latter's death. Thus did Saul depart this life.

[Antiquities 7:9:8, on Ahithophel]
Now Achitopel, when his proposal failed of acceptance, mounted his beast and set off for Gelmon his native city. And having called together all his people, he recounted to them the advice he had given Absalom, saying that, as Absalom had not followed it, he was clearly destined to perish before long, for David would conquer him and be restored to his throne. Therefore, he said, it was better to remove himself from the world in a free and noble spirit than surrender himself to David to be punished for having in all ways helped Absalom against him. After this speech he went into the innermost part of the house and hanged himself. Such was the death to which Achitopel, as his own judge, sentenced himself, and his relatives cut him down from the rope and gave him burial.

[Antiquities 8:12:5, on Zimri]
Zambrias seeing the city fall, fled to the innermost part of the palace and, setting it on fire, allowed himself to be consumed with it after a reign of only seven days.

Another important book by Josephus is The Jewish War, *which tells of the revolt against the Roman occupation of Palestine. Armed conflict broke out in A.D. 66 and ended in the destruction of Jerusalem in A.D. 70, and the final struggle that ended with the capture of Masada in A.D. 73. The Jewish state came to an end with these events. There are two separate excerpts from this lengthy book that are of direct concern to us.*

In A.D. 67 in Galilee, a battalion of Jewish rebels under the command of Josephus had been surrounded by the Romans and were on the point of being annihilated. His companions decide to commit suicide, but Josephus tries to dissuade them. This is the only instance in his writing where he denounces suicide. It is evident from his own account (3:8:7), he was not about to take this step himself no matter what the alternatives.

[War 3:8:5-7]

(5) Josephus, fearing an assault, and holding that it would be a betrayal of God's commands, should he die before delivering his message, proceeded, in this emergency, to reason philosophically with them.

"Why, comrades," said he "this thirst for our own blood? Why set asunder such fond companions as soul and body? . . .

"No; suicide is alike repugnant to that nature which all creatures share, and an act of impiety towards God who created us. Among the animals there is not one that deliberately seeks death or kills itself; so firmly rooted in all is nature's law—the will to live. That is why we account as enemies those who would openly take our lives and punish as assassins those who clandestinely attempt to do so. And God—think you not that he is indignant when man treats His gift with scorn? For it is from Him that we have received our being, and it is to Him that we should leave the decision to take it away. . . . Know you not that they who depart this life in accordance with the law of nature and repay the loan which they received from God, when He who lent is pleased to reclaim it, win eternal renown; that their house and families are secure; that their souls, remaining spotless and obedient, are allotted the most holy place in heaven, whence, in the revolution of the ages, they return to find in chaste bodies a new habitation? But as for those who have laid mad hands upon themselves, the darker regions of the nether world receive their souls, and God, their father, visits upon their posterity the outrageous acts of their parents. That is why this crime, so hateful to God, is punished also by the sagest of legislators. With us it is ordained that the body of a suicide should be exposed unburied until sunset, although it is thought right to bury even our enemies slain in war. In other nations the law requires that a suicide's right hand, with which he made war on himself, should be cut off, holding that, as the body was unnaturally severed from the soul, so the hand should be severed from the body.

"We shall do well then, comrades, to listen to reason and not to add to our human calamities the crime of impiety towards our creator. If our lives are offered us, let us live: there is nothing dishonorable in accepting this offer from those who have had so many proofs of our valor; if they think fit to kill us, death at the hands of our conquerors is honorable. But, for my part, I shall never pass over to the enemy's ranks, to prove a traitor to myself; I should indeed then be far more senseless than deserters who go over to the enemy for safety, whereas I should be going to destruction—my own destruction. I pray, however, that the Romans may prove faithless; if, after pledging their word, they put me to death, I shall die content, for I shall carry with me the consolation, better than a victory, that their triumph has been sullied by perjury."

(6) By these and many similar arguments Josephus sought to deter his companions from suicide. But desperation stopped their ears, for

they had long since devoted themselves to death. . . .

(7) [Josephus recognized he was not going to persuade them, so he proposed they draw lots to decide in which order they would die.] . . . . Each man thus selected presented his throat to his neighbor in the assurance that his general was forthwith to share his fate; for sweeter to them than life was the thought of death with Josephus. He, however (should one say by fortune or by the providence of God?), was left alone with one other; and anxious neither to be condemned by the lot nor, should he be left to the last, to stain his hand with the blood of a fellow-countryman, he persuaded this man also, under a pledge, to remain alive.

(8) Having thus survived the war with the Romans and that with his own friends, Josephus was brought by Nicanor into Vespasian's presence.

This next section is taken from the speech of Eliezar to the Zealots who were trapped in the Masada Fortress in A.D. 73 at the end of the Jewish revolt against the Romans.

[War 7:8:6-7:9:2]
(6) "I believe that it is God who has granted us this favor, that we have it in our power to die nobly and in freedom—a privilege denied to others who have met with unexpected defeat. Our fate at break of day is certain capture, but there is still the free choice of a noble death with those we hold most dear. . . . The penalty for those crimes let us pay not to our bitterest foes, the Romans, but to God through the act of our own hands. It will be more tolerable than the other. Let our wives thus die undishonored, our children unacquainted with slavery; and, when they are gone, let us render a generous service to each other, preserving our liberty as a noble winding-sheet. But first let us destroy our chattels and the fortress by the fire; for the Romans, well I know, will be grieved to lose at once our persons and the lucre. Our provisions only let us spare; for they will testify, when we are dead, that it was not want which subdued us, but that, in keeping with our initial resolve, we preferred death to slavery."

(7) ". . . deeply, indeed, was I deceived in thinking that I should have brave men as associates in our struggles for freedom—men determined to live with honor or to die. But you, it seems, were no better than the common herd in valor or in courage . . . for from of old, since the first dawn of intelligence, we have been continually taught by these precepts, ancestral and divine—confirmed by the deeds and noble spirit of our forefathers—that life, not death, is man's misfortune. For it is death which gives liberty to the soul and permits it to depart to its own pure abode, there to be free from all calamity; but so long as it is imprisoned in a mortal body and tainted with all its miseries, it is, in sober truth, dead, for association with what is mortal ill befits that which is divine. . . .

"Yet, even had we from the first been schooled in the opposite doctrine and taught that man's highest blessing is life and that death is a calamity, still the crisis is one that calls upon us to bear it with a stout heart, since it is by God's will and of necessity that we are to die. . . . Now that hope has vanished and left us alone in our distress, let us hasten to die honorably; let us have pity on ourselves, our children and our wives, while it is still in our power to find pity from ourselves. For we were born for death, we and those whom we have begotten; and this even the fortunate cannot escape. "

(9:1). . . having chosen by lot ten of their number to dispatch the rest, they laid themselves down each beside his prostrate wife and children, and, flinging their arms around them, offered their throats in readiness for the executants of the melancholy office. These, having unswervingly slaughtered all, ordained the same rule of the lot for one another, that he on whom it fell should slay first the nine and then himself last of all; such mutual confidence had they all that neither in acting nor in suffering would one differ from another. Finally, then, the nine bared their throats, and the last solitary survivor, after surveying the prostrate multitude, to see whether haply amid the shambles there were yet one left who needed his hand, and finding that all were slain, set the palace ablaze, and then collecting his strength drove his sword clean through his body and fell beside his family. They had died in the belief that they had left not a soul of them alive to fall into Roman hands; but an old woman and another, a relative of Eleazar, superior in sagacity and training to most of her sex, with five children, escaped by concealing themselves in the subterranean aqueducts, while the rest were absorbed in the slaughter. The victims numbered nine hundred and sixty, including women and children; and the tragedy occurred on the fifteenth of the month Xanthicus.

2 Maccabees 14:37-46 (*New English Bible*).

(37) A man called Razis, a member of the Jerusalem senate, was denounced to Nicanor [commander of the Elephant Corps under Demetrius, son of Seleucis]. He was very highly spoken of, a patriot who for his loyalty was known as 'Father of the Jews'. (38) In the early days of the secession he had stood his trial for practicing Judaism, and with the utmost eagerness had risked life and limb for the cause. (39) Nicanor wished to give clear proof of his hostility towards the Jews, and sent more that five hundred soldiers to arrest Razis; (40) he reckoned that his arrest would be a severe blow to the Jews. (41) The troops were on the point of capturing the tower where Razis was, and were trying to force the outer door. Then an order was given to set the door on fire, and Razis, hemmed in on all sides, turned his sword upon himself.

(42) He preferred to die nobly rather than fall into the hands of criminals and be subjected to gross humiliation. (43) In his haste and anxiety he misjudged the blow, and with the troops pouring through the doors he ran without hesitation on to the wall, and heroically threw himself down into the crowd. (44) The crowd hurriedly gave way, and he fell into the space they left. (45) He was still breathing, still on fire with courage; so streaming with blood and severely wounded, he picked himself up and dashed through the crowd. Finally, standing on a sheer rock, and now completely drained of blood (46) he took his entrails in both hands and flung them at the crowd. And thus, invoking the Lord of life and breath to give these entrails back to him again, he died.

4 Maccabees 16:24–17:6 *(New English Bible). The book known as 4 Maccabees probably comes from the area around Antioch in Syria. There is no agreement among scholars on the precise date of the book, except that it is most likely late first century or early second century AD. It is a discussion of the relative importance of "reason" and "passion," and is largely concerned with the heroic martyrdom of the Jews under the Seleucids. Chapters 8 to 18 tell of seven brothers who refused to bow to the pagan powers and were martyred. Their mother was steadfast in encouraging them to resist. We pick up the story at the end of chapter 16.*

(24) With these words the mother of the seven exhorted each one and persuaded them to die rather than transgress the commandment of God. (25) And they knew full well themselves that those who die for the sake of God live unto God, as do Abraham and Isaac and Jacob and all the patriarchs. (17:1) Some of the guards declared that when she, too, was about to be seized and put to death, she threw herself into the fire so that no one would touch her body. (2) O mother with the seven sons, who broke down the violence of the tyrant and thwarted his wicked devices and exhibited the nobility of faith! (3) Nobly set like a roof upon the pillars of your children, you sustained without yielding, the earthquake of the tortures. (4) Be of good cheer, therefore, mother of holy soul, whose hope of endurance is secure with God. (5) Not so majestic stands the moon in heaven as you stand, lighting the way to piety for your seven starlike sons, honored by God and firmly set with him in heaven. (6) For your childbearing was from our father Abraham.

Midrash Rabbah. *A Rabbinic document dated about A.D. 1000-1050 that preserves ancient interpretations of the Old Testament. Many of these traditions go back to the third and fourth centuries A.D.*

[Genesis Rabbah, "Noach" 34:13:2 (Genesis 9:5)].
And surely your blood of your lives I will require. This includes one who strangles himself. You might think that even one in the plight of Saul is meant: therefore we have *AK*. You might think, even one like Hananiah, Mishael, and Azariah: therefore we have *AK*.

[According to standard Rabbinic principles of interpretation, the word AK is understood to limit the previous argument. It provides an exception to the general rule just stated. "Therefore we have AK" indicates that the ones mentioned are not included in the category of those punished for shedding blood.

Hananiah, Mishael, and Azariah are the Hebrew names of Shadrach, Meshach, and Abednego, the three Jewish men thrown into the furnace by King Nebuchadnezzar of Babylon because they refused to worship the great golden idol the king had set up. The story is told in Daniel 1:6-7 and 3:1-30.]

[Leviticus Rabbah, "Emor" 26:7 (Leviticus 26:7), on Saul]
Our Rabbis learned: That righteous man [Saul] was slain because of five sins: as it says, *So Saul died for his transgression which he committed against the Lord* (1 Chronicles 10:13), and because he slew the inhabitants of Nob the city of the priests, and because he spared Agag, and because he did not obey Samuel—for it says: *Seven days shalt thou tarry until I come unto thee* (1 Samuel 10:8), and he did not do so—and because he inquired of the ghost and of the familiar spirit, *And inquired not of the Lord; therefore he slew him* (1 Chronicles 10:14). Hence it is written, *For the work of a man will He requite unto him, and cause every man to find according to his ways* (Job 34:11), and it is written, *A man also or a woman that divineth by a ghost or a familiar spirit, shall surely be put to death* (Leviticus 20:27).

Mishnah. *The Mishnah is the collection of traditional rabbinic interpretations and explanations of the Old Testament. Much of the material originates long before the time of Jesus and was preserved orally for many years. It was finally put into written form by Rabbi Judah ha-Nasi and his followers about the beginning of the third century (A.D. 200).*

[Aboth 4:22]
The born are destined to die, the dead to be brought to life, and the living to be judged; it is therefore, for them to know and to make known, so that it becomes known that He is God. He the fashioner, He the creator, He the discerner, He the judge, He the witness, He the complainant, and that He is of a certainty to judge, blessed be He before whom there is no unrighteousness, nor forgetting, nor respect of persons, nor taking

of bribes, for all is his. And know that all is according to the reckoning. And let not thy evil inclination assure thee that the grave is a place of refuge for thee, for without thy will wast thou fashioned, without thy will wast thou born, without thy will livest thou, without thy will wilt thou die, and without thy will art thou of a certainty to give an account and reckoning before the King of Kings, blessed be He.

[Sanhedrin 11:1-2]
All Israelites have a share in the world to come. . . . And these are they that have no share in the world to come: he that says there is no resurrection of the dead [prescribed in the Law]; and [he that says] that the Law is not from heaven, and an Epicurean. [Translator's note: "A frequent epithet applied to both Gentiles and Jews opposed to the rabbinic teachings. It is in no way associated with the teachings supposed by the Jews to emanate from the philosopher Epicurus; to Jewish ears it conveys the sense of the root *pakar* 'to be free from restraint,' and so licentious and skeptical."] Rabbi Akiba says: Also he that reads heretical books [note: "Literally 'external books,' books excluded from the canon of Hebrew Scripture."] or that utters charms over a wound . . . Abba Saul says: Also he that pronounces the Name with its proper letters. . . . Three kings and four commoners have no share in the world to come. The three kings are Jeroboam [1 Kings 12:25–14:20], and Ahab [1 Kings 16:29-34; 18:1–22:40], and Manasseh [2 Kings 21:1-18] . . . the four commoners are Balaam [Num. 22:1–24:25], and Doeg [1 Sam. 21:7; 22:11-23], and Ahithophel [2 Sam. 17:1-23], and Gehazi [2 Kings 5:19-27].

In both the Babylonian Talmud *(Sanhedrin 11) and the* Jerusalem Talmud *(Sanhedrin 10) there is extensive discussion of this passage from the* Mishnah. *The material runs to nearly 140 pages in the* Babylonian Talmud *and gets very involved with elaborate examination of what appears to the modern reader to be totally irrelevant details. Out of the interminable discussion, the following summary judgments on these seven emerge: They have no share in the life to come because:*

Jeroboam "debased the nation with the golden calf." He was "the first to corrupt Israel."

Ahab "denied the God of Israel," therefore "he has no portion in the God of Israel."

Manasseh "forgot God," and "shed innocent blood" (i.e. killed the prophets) and "made a grove as Ahab did" (i.e. became an idolater).

Balaam "because of bestiality" and because he "practiced enchantment."

Doeg "forgot his learning."

Ahithophel "betrayed his teacher" (David).

Gehazi because he was unrepentant and a leper.

One other reference to suicide in the Talmud *is in the tractate "Abodah Zarah " in what is called "the incident about Beruia." The incident as related in* Kiddushim *80b is to the effect that when Rabbi Meir's wife taunted him about the familiar rabbinic adage 'Women are light-minded,' he replied that she herself would testify to its truth. When, subsequently, she was enticed by one of her husband's disciples, she indeed proved to be too weak to resist. She then committed suicide, and her husband for shame, ran away to Babylon.*

Pliny, *Letters.* **Pliny the Younger (A.D. 61-114), held a number of important legal and administrative posts in the Roman government from about A.D. 80 until his death in 113 or 114. In 110 or 111 he was appointed as personal representative of the Emperor Trajan to Bithynia in Asia Minor with full power to restore order and stability to that troubled province. His correspondence with the Emperor provides valuable insight into the working of the Imperial government.**

[96, "To the Emperor Trajan"]

It is a rule, Sir, which I inviolably observe, to refer myself to you in all my doubts; for who is more capable of guiding my uncertainty or informing my ignorance? Having never been present at any trials of Christians, I am unacquainted with the method and limits to be observed either in examining or punishing them. Whether any difference is to be made on account of age, or no distinction allowed between the youngest and the adult; whether repentance admits to a pardon, or if a man has been once a Christian it avails him nothing to recant; whether the mere profession of Christianity, albeit without crimes, or only the crimes associated therewith are punishable—in all these points I am greatly doubtful.

In the meanwhile, the method I have observed towards those who have been denounced to me as Christians is this: I interrogated them whether they were Christians; if they confessed it I repeated the question twice again, adding the threat of capital punishment; if they still persevered, I ordered them to be executed. For whatever the nature of their creed might be, I could at least feel no doubt that contumacy and inflexible obstinacy deserved chastisement. There were others also possessed of the same infatuation, but being citizens of Rome, I directed them to be carried thither.

These accusations spread (as is usually the case) from the mere fact of the matter being investigated and several forms of mischief came to light. A placard was put up, without any signature, accusing a large number of persons by name. Those who denied they were, or ever had been, Christians, who repeated after me an invocation to the gods, and offered adoration, with wine and frankincense, to your image, which I had ordered to be brought for the purpose, together with those of the gods, and who finally cursed Christ—none of which acts, it is said, those who are really Christians can be forced into performing—these I thought it proper to discharge. Others who were named by that informer at first confessed themselves Christians, and then denied it; true, they had been of that persuasion but they had quitted it, some three years, other many years, and a few as much as twenty-five years ago. They all worshipped your statue and the images of the gods, and cursed Christ.

They affirmed, however, the whole of their guilt, or their error, was, that they were in the habit of meeting on a certain fixed day before it was light, when they sang in alternate verses a hymn to Christ, as to a god, and bound themselves by a solemn oath, not to any wicked deeds, but never to commit any fraud, theft or adultery, never to falsify their word, nor deny a trust when they should be called upon to deliver it up; after which it was their custom to separate, and then reassemble to partake of food—but food of an ordinary and innocent kind. Even this practice, however, they had abandoned after the publication of my edict, by which, according to your orders, I had forbidden political associations. I judged it so much the more necessary to extract the real truth, with the assistance of torture, from two female slaves, who were styled *deaconesses:* but I could discover nothing more than depraved and excessive superstition.

I therefore adjourned the proceedings, and betook myself at once to your counsel. For the matter seemed to me well worth referring to you—especially considering the numbers endangered. Persons of all ranks and ages, and of both sexes are, and will be, involved in the prosecution. For this contagious superstition is not confined to the cities only, but has spread through the villages and rural districts; it seems possible, however, to check and cure it. 'Tis certain at least that the temples, which had been almost deserted, begin now to be frequented; and the sacred festivals, after a long intermission, are again revived; while there is a general demand for sacrificial animals, which for some time past have met with but few purchasers. From hence it is easy to imagine what multitudes may be reclaimed from this error, if a door be left open to repentance.

[97, "Trajan to Pliny"]

The method you have pursued, my dear Pliny, in sifting the cases of those denounced to you as Christians is extremely proper. It is not possible to lay down any general rule which can be applied as the fixed standard in all cases of this nature. No search should be made for these people; when they are denounced and found guilty they must be punished; with the restriction, however, that when the party denies himself to be a Christian, and shall give proof that he is not (that is, by adoring our gods) he shall be pardoned on the ground of repentance, even though he may have formerly incurred suspicion. Informations without the accuser's name subscribed must not be admitted in evidence against anyone, as it is introducing a very dangerous precedent, and by no means agreeable to the spirit of the age.

Seneca. *(A Roman Stoic philosopher who lived about A.D. 50-130).*

[Epistle 70, "On the Proper Time to Slip the Cable," sections 4-6]
For mere living is not a good, but living well. Accordingly, the wise man will live as long as he ought, not as long as he can. He will mark in what place, with whom, and how he is to conduct his existence, and what he is about to do. He always reflects concerning the quality, and not the quantity, of his life. As soon as there are many events in his life that give him trouble and disturb his peace of mind, he sets himself free. And this privilege is his, not only when the crisis is upon him, but as soon as Fortune seems to be playing him false; then he looks about carefully and sees whether he ought, or ought not, to end his life on that account. He holds that it makes no difference to him whether his taking-off be natural or self-inflicted, whether it comes later or earlier. He does not regard it with fear, as if it were a great loss; for no man can lose very much when but a driblet remains. It is not a question of dying earlier or later, but of dying well or ill. And dying well means escape from the danger of living ill.

[Sections 11-13]
No general statement can be made, therefore, with regard to the question whether, when a power beyond our control threatens us with death, we should anticipate death, or await it. For there are many arguments to pull us in either direction. If one death is accompanied by torture, and the other is simple and easy, why not snatch the latter? Just as I select my ship when I am about to go on a voyage, or my house when I propose to take a residence, so I shall choose my death when I am about to depart from life. Moreover, just as a long-drawn-out life does not necessarily mean a better one, so a long-drawn-out death necessarily means a worse one. There is no occasion when the soul should be humored more than at the moment of death. Let the soul depart as it feels itself impelled to go; whether it seeks the sword or the halter, or some draught that attacks the veins, let it proceed and burst the bonds of its slavery. Every man ought to make his life acceptable to others besides himself, but his death to himself alone. The best form of death is the one we like.

[Section 15]

The best thing which eternal law ever ordained was that it allowed to us one entrance into life, but many exits. Must I await the cruelty either of disease or of man, when I can depart through the midst of torture, and shake off my troubles. This is the one reason why we cannot complain of life: it keeps no one against his will. Humanity is well situated, because no man is unhappy except by his own fault. Live, if you so desire; if not, you may return to the place whence you came.

[Epistle 77, "On Taking One's Own Life," sections 3-4]

For however small my possessions might be, I should still have left over more travelling-money than journey to travel, especially since this journey upon which we have set out is one which need not be followed to the end. An expedition will be incomplete if one stops half-way, or anywhere on this side of one's destination; but life is not incomplete if it is honorable. At whatever point you leave off living, provided you leave off nobly, your life is a whole. Often, however, one must leave off bravely, and our reasons therefore need not be momentous; for neither are the reasons momentous which hold us here.

[Sections 10-13]

There are times when we ought to die and are unwilling; sometimes we die and are unwilling. No one is so ignorant as not to know that we must at some time die; nevertheless, when one draws near death, one turns to flight, trembles, and laments. Would you not think him an utter fool who wept because he was not alive a thousand years ago? And is he not just as much a fool who weeps because he will not be alive a thousand years from now? It is all the same; you will not be, and you were not. Neither of these periods of time belongs to you. You have been cast upon this point of time; if you would make it longer, how much longer shall you make it? Why weep? Why pray? You are taking pains to no purpose.

> Give over thinking that your prayers can bend
> Divine decrees from their predestined end.
> (Vergil, *Æneid*, 6:376)

These decrees are unalterable and fixed; they are governed by a mighty and everlasting compulsion. Your goal will be the goal of all things. What is there strange in this to you? You were born to be subject to this law; this fate befell your father, your mother, your ancestors, all who came before you; and it will befall all who shall come after you. A sequence which cannot be broken or altered by any power binds all things together, and draws all things in its course. Think of the multitudes of men doomed to death who will come after you, of the multitudes who will go with you! You would die more bravely, I suppose, in the company of many thousands, and yet there are many thousands, both of men and animals, who at this very moment, while you are irresolute about death are breathing their last, in their several ways. But you—did you believe that you would not some day reach the goal towards which you have always been traveling? No journey but has its end.

[Sections 18-20]
You are afraid of death; but how can you scorn it in the midst of a mushroom supper? You wish to live; well, do you know how to live? You are afraid to die. But come now: is this life of yours anything but death? . . . "But," says one, "I wish to live, for I am engaged in many honorable pursuits. I am loth to leave life's duties, which I am fulfilling with loyalty and zeal." Surely you are aware that dying is also one of life's duties? You are deserting no duty, for there is no definite number established which you are bound to complete. There is no life that is not short. . . . It is with life as it is with a play—it matters not how long the action is spun out, but how good the acting is. It makes no difference at what point you stop. Stop whenever you choose; only see to it that the closing period is well turned.

Although there is a lot of material on suicide, there has not been much written from a Christian perspective. And most of the literature tends to concentrate on research into the causes of suicide or of case studies of attempted or successful suicides. There is next to nothing on the problems of coping with the aftermath. However, these books and articles may be helpful for those who want to pursue the topic beyond what has been offered in the Appendix.

Amery, Jean. *Discourses on Suicide.* Translated by John D. Barlow. Bloomington, Ind.: Indiana University Press, 1999.

Anderson, S. J. *When Someone Wants to Die.* Downers Grove, Ill.: InterVarsity Press, 1988.

Bailey, Lloyd R. *Biblical Perspectives on Death.* Philadelphia: Fortress, 1979.

Barth, Karl. *Church Dogmatics.* Vol. 3. Part 4. Edinburgh: T. & T. Clark, 1961.

Bayet, M. Albert. *Suicide and Morality.* Salem, N.H.: Arno, 1975.

Bloom, Lois A. *Mourning After Suicide.* New York: Pilgrim, 1985.

Bonhoeffer, Dietrich. *Ethics.* London: SCM Press, 1971, see especially pages 141-47.

Colt, George Howe. *The Enigma of Suicide.* New York: Simon & Schuster, 1991.

Daube, David. "Death as Release in the Bible." *Novum Testamentum* 5 (1962): 82-104.

Donne, John. *Biathanatos (Suicide).* New York: Garland, 1982.

Droge, Arthur J. "*Mori Lucrum*: Paul and Ancient Theories of Suicide." *Novum Testamentum* 30 (1988): 263-86.

Durkheim, Emile. *Suicide.* New York: Macmillan, 1951.

Elrid, John. *Caring for the Suicidal.* London: Constable, 1988.

Frend, W. H. C. *Martyrdom and Persecution in the Early Church.* Oxford: Blackwell, 1965.

Gernsbacker, Larry M. *The Suicide Syndrome.* New York: Human Sciences, 1985.

Gese, Hartmut. "Death in the Old Testament." In *Essays on Biblical Theology*, 34-59. Minneapolis: Augsburg, 1981.

Harding, Michael. "The Liberation of Dying." *Theology* (July 1982): 243-46.

Hsu, Albert Y. *Grieving a Suicide*. Downers Grove, Ill.: InterVarsity Press, 2002.

Landsberg, Paul Louis. *The Moral Problem of Suicide*. London: Rockliff, 1953.

Linzer, Norman, ed. *Suicide: The Will to Live vs. the Will to Die*. New York: Human Sciences, 1984.

McIntosh, John L. *Research on Suicide: A Bibliography*. London: Greenwood, 1985.

Moore, Charles. *A Full Inquiry into the Subject of Suicide*. London, 1790.

Pohier, J., and D. Mieth, eds. *Suicide and the Right to Die*. (*Concilium* 179) Edinburgh: T. & T. Clark, 1985.

Rosner, Fred. "Suicide in Biblical, Talmudic, and Rabbinic Writings." *Tradition* 11 (1970): 25-40.

Thielicke, Helmut. *Living with Death*. Grand Rapids: Eerdmans, 1983.

White, John. *The Masks of Melancholy: A Christian Psychiatrist Looks at Depression and Suicide*. Downers Grove, Ill.: InterVarsity Press, 1982.

Wolsterstorff, Nicholas. *Lament for a Son*. Grand Rapids: Eerdmans, 1987.

Appendix Bibliography

Ambrose. *Selected Works and Letters: A Select Library of Nicene and Post-Nicene Fathers of the Christian Church*. Second Series. Translated by H. De Romestin. Vol. 10. Oxford: James Parker, 1896.

Aquinas, Thomas. *Summa Theologica*. London: Burns, Oates & Washbourne, 1929.

Aristotle. *The Nicomachean Ethics*. Translated by H. Rackham. Cambridge, Mass.: Harvard University Press, 1926.

Augustine. *The City of God: The Works of Aurelius Augustine*. Edited and translated by Marcus Dods. Vol 1. Edinburgh: T. & T. Clark, 1871.

Epictetus. *The Discourses*. Translated by W. A. Oldfather. Cambridge, Mass.: Harvard University Press, 1928.

Epstein, Isadore, trans. and ed. *The Babylonian Talmud*. 18 vols. London: Soncino, 1961.

Freedman, H. and Maurice Simon, eds. *Midrash Rabbah*. 10 vols. London: Soncino, 1939.

Josephus. *The Antiquities of the Jews*. Translated by H. St J. Thackery. Cambridge, Mass.: Harvard University Press, 1927.

Josephus. *The Jewish War*. Translated by H. St J. Thackery. Cambridge, Mass.: Harvard University Press, 1927.

Lightfoot, J. B. *The Apostolic Fathers: Revised Texts with Short Introductions and English Translations*. London: Macmillan, 1893.

Neusner, Jacob, trans. *Genesis Rabbah: The Judaic Commentary to the Book of Genesis: A New American Translation in three volumes.* Atlanta: Scholars Press, 1985.

Pliny. *Letters*. Translated by William Melmoth. Revised by W. M. L. Hutchinson. Cambridge, Mass.: Harvard University Press, 1924.

Seneca. *Epistulae Morales (Letters to Lucilius)*. Translated by R. M. Gummere. Cambridge, Mass.: Harvard University Press, 1970).

Index of Names and Subjects

Index of Bible references

G. Lloyd Carr is professor emeritus of biblical studies at Gordon College. He is the author of *Song of Solomon*, a Tyndale Old Testament Commentary, for which he won the 1985 Evangelical Christian Publishers Association Gold Medallion Book Award. His work has appeared in many scholarly journals, encyclopedias, dictionaries, and other collections.

Gwendolyn Carr, a poet and professional dressmaker and designer, is published widely in magazines and journals. She is the author of two books.